PRAISE FOR *HOW DID I GET HERE?*

"It's a time of upheaval. All of us feel a little shaky and Christine Caine steadies our anxious doubts. God is real. He is coming and our hope is secure. This book will bring you back to a faith that is full and alive again."

—Jennie Allen, founder and visionary of IF: Gathering and *New York Times* bestselling author of *Get Out of Your Head*

"Through her own deeply personal stories, Christine pours out wisdom onto her readers once again. In *How Did I Get Here?* she reminds us that there is a little bit of doubt in all of us, but she lovingly guides us through and encourages us to get honest with God."

—Roma Downey, Emmy-nominated actress, producer, and *New York Times* bestselling author

"If you know how it feels for everything around you to be okay while nothing inside you is, this book is for you. If you honestly don't want to keep going but you *want* to want to, this book is for you. If you need a triumphant, trauma-scarred leader to give you a glimpse of your next, Christine is the woman for the job and this book is for you. *How Did I Get Here?* will fill you with soul-anchoring hope. This book is for you."

—Dr. Anita Phillips, trauma therapist and host of *In the Light* podcast

"Christine's book, *How Did I Get Here?* is like an honest conversation with a friend and mentor. Through her biblical insight and humor, she helps you recognize the patterns and areas of your life that are leading you away from the things of God—and then shows you how to shift your eyes back to him. As a personal mentor of mine, I can attest to the godly wisdom that Christine carries—and I know everyone who picks up this book will have an encounter with Jesus."

—Sadie Robertson Huff, author, speaker, and founder of Live Original

"Christine Caine's relentless pursuit to take the hope of Jesus to the world is deeply effective in her new book *How Did I Get Here?* She asks intimate questions that all of our hearts know well and points the wandering soul back home with compassion and strength. We thank God for Christine and her example in our lives as a leader, activist, teacher, and follower of Jesus. This book will encourage your life profoundly!"

—Rich Wilkerson Jr., lead pastor of VOUS Church

"Raw. Vulnerable. Honest. If you've reached a place where you've stopped hoping, stopped dreaming, or stopped praying . . . if things around you are flourishing and alive, but inside you're anything but, if you feel like you may bend and break, this book is a map, showing you how to put the pieces back together."

—Paula Faris, journalist, author, and podcaster

HOW DID
I GET
HERE?

ALSO BY CHRISTINE CAINE

Undaunted

Unstoppable

Unashamed

Unexpected

Unshakeable

HOW DID I GET HERE?

Finding Your Way Back to God When
Everything Is Pulling You Away

CHRISTINE CAINE

NELSON
BOOKS

An Imprint of Thomas Nelson

Published in Nashville, Tennessee, by Nelson Books, an imprint of Thomas Nelson. Nelson Books and Thomas Nelson are registered trademarks of HarperCollins Christian Publishing, Inc.

Published in association with Yates & Yates, www.yates2.com.

Thomas Nelson titles may be purchased in bulk for educational, business, fundraising, or sales promotional use. For information, please email SpecialMarkets@ThomasNelson.com.

ISBN 978-1-4002-2656-6 (HC)
ISBN 978-1-4002-3000-6 (ITPE)
ISBN 978-1-4002-2658-0 (eBook)
ISBN 978-0-310-13267-7 (Custom)

Library of Congress Cataloging-in-Publication Data

Names: Caine, Christine, 1966- author.
Title: How did I get here?: finding your way back to God when everything is pulling you away / Christine Caine.
Description: Nashville, Tennesse: Nelson Books, [2021] | Includes bibliographical references.
Summary: "Bestselling author, speaker, and activist Christine Caine helps readers who are feeling weary and like things somehow aren't quite right to identify how they ended up where they are and what they need to do to course-correct and anchor themselves in the only One who does not change or shift with the currents"-- Provided by publisher.
Identifiers: LCCN 2020051543 (print) | LCCN 2020051544 (ebook) | ISBN 9781400226566 (hardcover) | ISBN 9781400226580 (epub)
Subjects: LCSH: Fortitude. | Mental fatigue--Religious aspects--Christianity. | Perseverance (Theology) | Encouragement--Religious aspects--Christianity. | Christian life.
Classification: LCC BV4647.F6 C35 2021 (print) | LCC BV4647.F6 (ebook) | DDC 248.4--dc23
LC record available at https://lccn.loc.gov/2020051543
LC ebook record available at https://lccn.loc.gov/2020051544

Printed in the United States of America

21 22 23 24 25   LSC   10 9 8 7 6 5 4 3 2 1

To my darling Nick,

Jesus is the anchor of my soul, especially when the wind and the waves want to take me off course, but you have been the stabilizing force in my life. I like to think of you as the gyrostabilizer of our boat as we sail through our time on this earth—that engineering feat that keeps it all afloat. How many times a day, through all the years of our life and ministry together, have you kept everything running and our boat from capsizing? You, Nick, are the one who keeps it all upright, on course, and moving full steam ahead. You are the ballast of our family's life.

For this, and reasons a million more, I love you.

For this reason, we must pay attention all the more to what we have heard, so that we will not drift away.

—HEBREWS 2:1

CONTENTS

INTRODUCTION

When I Wanted to Ring the Bell of Defeat

If you want to change the world, don't ever, ever ring
the bell.

—ADMIRAL WILLIAM H. MCRAVEN

For months, I tossed and turned. From side to side. From front
to back. I plumped my pillow. I flattened my pillow. I piled on
the covers. I threw them off. I stared into the darkness, my mind
often locked in an endless cycle of thinking, fighting not to think,
then landing in an emptiness that quickly refilled with flash-
backs . . . of shifts I had seen coming and ones I didn't . . . of new
beginnings I had managed to control and endings I couldn't . . .
of narratives I wanted to rewrite so badly. I knew that rehashing
the past couple of years would never make sense of the desperate
feelings I was facing. But I also couldn't get away from what I
was feeling. I was eager to rid myself of the turmoil, the chaos,
the noise—just long enough to find some sort of peace, so I could

sleep. Eventually, I would give up and get up. Night after night. At home. In hotel rooms. In every time zone.

So many nights I wanted to wake Nick. To talk it out. To try and figure it out. But there really wasn't anything new to say. He was such a faithful husband and friend, and he had listened to me hash it out, dig it out, desperately trying to unravel whatever was in knots. He was well aware and faithfully praying for me. There was no sense in robbing him of his sleep. We didn't both need to be awake.

This new season—this unwanted and unwelcome season— was unlike any previous season of my life. I've always been someone who has soldiered on. Stirred up my faith. Passionately pursued every new frontier. Thrived on being on the cutting edge of whatever God was doing and wherever he was going. But something had changed. Not just around me. In me. And I was unable to sort it all out.

Truthfully, deep down, I knew sleep wasn't really what I wanted most. I wanted answers. But in the moment, I needed rest even more than answers—though it was tempting to think answers would give me rest.

Still, I *wanted* answers. My mind *needed* answers. I wasn't used to having an undercurrent of feeling unsettled, of there being something I couldn't quite put my finger on.

For weeks I had tried exhausting myself at the gym. Going for a run. A bike ride. A swim. Anything to get myself off the mental treadmill threatening to overtake me. All to no avail.

Then one night, Nick suggested we watch a TV show. To relax before bed, he said. Only, he picked another one of those documentaries he loves to watch. I couldn't imagine how that could possibly help, but nothing I'd tried thus far had worked, so what did I have to lose? That evening's feature was an inside view of the most treacherous week United States Navy SEAL recruits endure to pass their training and be awarded the elite honor of calling themselves SEALs. The challenge is known as Hell Week.

Nick was all in from the beginning, but I was slower to engage. Perhaps if it had been *G.I. Jane*, the 1997 action-packed film starring Demi Moore, I could have been more on board. There would have been a suspenseful plot, a tense conflict, and finally a resolution leaving me with a boatload of winning emotions—and one iconic American hero. Jane would have inspired me to kick some serious Devil butt. Granted, it would probably have wound me up rather than down.

Nick's choice wasn't exactly riveting. Characteristic of documentaries, it was narrated. All the way through. By a calming monotone voice. Setting my phone aside, I chose to give it a fair shot. Five minutes in, to my surprise, skepticism gave way to curiosity, and before I knew it, I was intrigued.

There was something about the recruits' journey that began to tug at me. For days they are made to feel wet, cold, and exhausted. Lugging logs over their heads, treading water, jumping out of helicopters into more water, being rained on with shovels of sand. They crawl on shore, only to be dragged back out to sea, then hauled back to land, and left disoriented. Confused. Fighting to focus. Fighting to stay awake. They are forced to push their muscles past levels of pain that fade into numb. Some of the most brilliant and physically fit military personnel on the planet, they are demoralized in every way possible in order to reach a breaking point mentally and emotionally. And most of them do break. More than half of them cave. But that's the point. Better to break on a beach in California than on a mission in a volatile part of the world.

To make their training even more brutal, a shiny, gold bell is always strategically placed in their line of sight. At any point in the training, just by ringing it three times, they can end their hardship. They can rescue themselves from the most grueling training on earth. No questions asked.

Ring the bell, and they no longer have to wake up at five o'clock—or endure sleeplessness altogether. Ring the bell, and they no longer have to brave the freezing cold swims in utter blackness. Ring the bell, and they no longer have to roll in the sand and be a "sugar cookie." Ring the bell, and they can be freed from the pain of it all.

In one minute—literally in just one minute—they can change the trajectory of their entire destiny. By ringing the bell, they can find themselves transported at once from suffering to standing in a hot shower or putting on dry, clean clothes or eating a hot meal. Ending their misery can be that quick. That easy. They can tap out and go back to their familiar posts in the military and home to their families—letting go once and forevermore the dream of becoming a Navy SEAL.

Watching their vicious fight to deny their physical condition, to rise above it mentally, to overcome intentional and insurmountable odds, left me wanting to ring the bell for them.

And . . . for me.

No sooner did I have that realization than the deep-seated storm of emotion inside of me began to swell. Until that moment, I hadn't known how to describe the relentless angst in my heart and mind. I reached for my chest, trying to steady myself. The feelings that had been stalking me, drawing closer and closer until they felt like they were jumping out at me when I least expected, surprised me once more—and left me deeply troubled.

Being surprised brings on a whole range of emotions I've never managed well. Even when it's a good surprise like a birthday party. For some reason, those are the worst. I've been told this stems from feelings and fragments of trauma left from the abandonment and abuse I experienced as a child. Suffice it to say, I like knowns. Not unknowns.

These troubled feelings, this tugging of anxiety, had been an unknown. Something to be explored or unraveled. But watching the SEAL recruits ring the bell, one after another, started to bring understanding, at least in part. Something had revealed itself. Something had poked its head up and snuck a peek at me—and I had caught a glimpse of it.

I turned to Nick, unable to stop the tears from tumbling. "I think I'm beginning to understand the last two years. I feel like I've been dropped out of a helicopter, left sitting in the cold, cold water, and I've been there for six hours, but I'm required to endure for eight. My brain knows I can keep going. My heart knows I can keep going. I know that I can actually stay in this freezing cold water another two hours. I know it's not going to kill me. I've lived long enough to know Jesus will sustain me. I've been trained, I'm physically fit, I'm called by God, I have the ability. I know what is required of me to keep going, and for the first time in my ministry life, I don't know if I *want* to. I literally don't know if I *want* to keep going. I think I want to ring the bell."

Have you ever said something and felt all the air leave your lungs with the last syllable of your sentence? That's what happened for me. Wrapping words around the angst that had been prowling around me for months shook me to my core like nothing ever had. It scared me in a way I'd never known. There had been moments in my life when I wanted to walk away—temporarily.

Moments when I'd felt deeply betrayed, deeply disillusioned, deeply hurt, deeply disappointed, deeply flawed, deeply misrepresented, deeply discouraged, deeply misunderstood. But never had I hit a wall where I thought, *I don't know if I actually want to keep going.*

I couldn't hide my own shock. And I couldn't help but wonder, *How did I get here?*

BUT EVERYTHING WAS FLOURISHING

I thought I was strong because I had always been strong. For more than thirty years I had been pursuing Jesus with a passion, following wherever he led me with great gratitude and commitment. I had never forgotten what my life was like when he found me or all he had done for me in the years since. But make no mistake, it had been a costly journey—mentally, emotionally, physically, personally, spiritually . . .

- When my family didn't understand my decision to surrender my life to Jesus.
- When I had to say goodbye to some relationships to follow Jesus.
- When I walked away from a thriving career to answer the call to ministry.
- When I was the only woman leading in a ministry setting.
- When I had a huge dream and few resources.
- When it felt like I was all alone.
- When I was single and everyone I knew was married.

- When Nick and I married and could barely make ends meet.
- When we had a child, lost a child, and then had another.
- When we traveled to the nations to preach the gospel and lived unsettled and unrooted for weeks at a time.
- When we moved our family from one continent to another.
- When we chose to launch a global anti–trafficking organization—A21.
- When we started a women's leadership initiative—Propel.
- When I said yes to a television program that would reach the world—*Equip & Empower.*

It all had cost more than we ever anticipated, but the fruit was stunning. God had exceeded our every hope and expectation. He had been so gracious to us, so faithful, so kind. By the time we celebrated twenty-one years of marriage and ministry, everything was flourishing—everything except me.

I should have been on top of the world, but I wasn't. I should have been enjoying the fruit of my labor, but I wasn't. I should have been full of peace and joy, but I wasn't. I should have been full of vision for the future, but I wasn't. Something was off, and until that night, I could not quite pinpoint exactly what it was.

I was grateful to have a glimpse of clarity, albeit from a documentary, but now that I had some language to wrap around my feelings, I desperately wanted more understanding. The realization that I wasn't sure I wanted what I had always wanted the way I had wanted it was startling. Did I really feel that what had always been worthwhile suddenly wasn't? Was I actually questioning whether I wanted to keep following Jesus wherever he would lead me? Surely not, but I was definitely in a place I had never imagined.

I didn't know if I wanted to keep pressing in and pressing on. Reaching out for the next thing. Pursuing the adventure I had always chased. It wasn't a crisis of faith; rather, it was a sober realization that if I were to keep going, it would probably mean more sacrifice, more pain, more heartache, more exposure, more vulnerability, more attacks . . . even though all of that would mean more fruit.

The course Jesus had charted for me was worthy of my continuing—because Jesus was worthy of my continuing—but somewhere I had drifted from seeing that to losing myself in my feelings. And my feelings were screaming at me to ring the bell. I mean, I knew that I could keep going through the motions, and no one would really know I wasn't pressing in as hard as I once was, sticking as close to Jesus as I once did. Willing to keep taking risks as I always had. I could be just like the recruit who rings the bell and doesn't get to be a SEAL but is still in the military. Still one of the strongest and bravest. Still honorable and dutiful, serving his country. No one would know I rang the bell. Except Jesus. And his knowing mattered more than anything.

Maybe my beleaguered state was from all the years of being on the front line. Of pioneering. Of daring to go where no one else was going. Of relentless spiritual warfare. Maybe it was from running full steam ahead. Or from feeling exposed, raw, vulnerable, and sometimes like an easy target. Maybe it was caused by the failure of a project I had poured my heart and soul into. Maybe I was still being affected from losing my mum and three other family members the year before. Maybe the loss of intimacy in letting go of some friendships I had treasured, ones that had fractured, left me feeling hurt and misunderstood, perhaps even jaded. It had been a huge season of loss on so many levels.

But don't we all deal with being hit by compounding blows? Don't we all lose loved ones? Don't we all grow weary in our callings and careers? Don't we all experience disappointments? And struggle with being disillusioned? Don't we all want to walk away from time to time?

Truth be told, I've lost count of the number of times I thought of walking away from it all and opening a small café in Santorini, Greece. Just Nick and me and our girls tucked away in my favorite corner of the world. Can't you picture me suggesting another cup of coffee to go with your baklava? I imagine we all run to our own little escape destinations in our minds. To the lives we thought we might have but never will. Because deep down we love Jesus and his plans more.

Instead of letting myself go there this time, I turned and faced the journey ahead of me—one I had never anticipated. I found myself in a place where I wanted to take cover more than I wanted to take ground. Where I didn't feel that I had the strength, courage, or confidence to keep going. And yet, at the same time, I knew I would. Jesus had always been the anchor of my soul, so I would find what I needed where I always had—in him.

> I found myself in a place where I wanted to take cover more than I wanted to take ground.

PAY ATTENTION

And he did not disappoint. He did not leave me abandoned or unaided. He never has. He never will. A few afternoons later, while I was reading the book of Hebrews, words that I had read many times before seemed to jump off the page.

> Therefore we must *pay much closer attention* to what we have heard, *lest we drift* away from it. For since the message declared by angels proved to be reliable, and every transgression or disobedience received a just retribution, how shall we escape if we neglect such a great salvation? It was declared at first by the Lord, and it was attested to us by those who heard, while God also bore witness by signs and wonders and various miracles and by gifts of the Holy Spirit distributed according to his will. (Heb. 2:1–4 ESV, emphasis mine)

Pay much closer attention.

Lest we drift.

All of a sudden, I had a thought: *Perhaps this is how I found myself wanting to ring the bell. Have I quit paying close attention? If so, to what? Have I drifted? If so, from what?*

"Pay attention, pay much closer attention." I had heard words of warning like this before. All throughout my childhood. I learned to speak Greek before I spoke English, and my mother always spoke to us in Greek. When she wanted to really get something across to my two brothers and me, she would use the same words as the writer of Hebrews: *perissoteros prosechein.* When she spoke these words, she was telling us to be careful and pay *extra* attention. Her tone would be urgent, serious, instructive, and commanding of our focus—especially when she was sharing about something critical to our well-being, like when she taught us to look both ways before running after a ball that had rolled into the street. Or when she wanted us to stay put on a bench and be safe while she tended to some business at a bank or in a store.

Perissoteros prosechein.

She said it when we learned to ride our bikes. Walk to school. Run across the neighborhood to a friend's house.

Perissoteros prosechein.

"Pay extra attention," my mother said.

"Pay extra attention," the writer of Hebrews said.

Why pay extra attention? *Lest you drift.* It's as though the writer knew the more familiar we became, the less attention we would pay—to God, his Word, and his ways. The more we learned, the more likely we would take it all for granted—and miss the awe of our salvation.

Pay attention.

Lest you drift.

IT'S SO EASY TO DRIFT

I know about drifting. My dad drilled the dangers of it into me when I was just a kid. Every year, he and Mum would take us kids on an annual trip to Umina Beach, just an hour's drive north of Sydney, where we lived. It was a great getaway we all looked forward to, but we always seemed to go when the pelicans were more populous than the swimmers. That meant we were guaranteed to get pelican itch from swimming in the water—so Mum always faithfully packed the calamine lotion. It sounds gross, and if you google pictures, it looks gross, but apart from giving us a head-to-toe rash and making us itch, it was harmless.

Going for a summer holiday also meant swimming against a

strong undertow. Knowing that we could be swept out to sea, my dad coached us every year about the dangers of the undercurrent and what to do if we felt ourselves being pulled under or away from the shore.

Then, once we were out on the beach, he had a routine for keeping us safe. He would set up an umbrella in the sand—always one so vivid I felt sure everyone on the beach knew we had to be Greek. Other families had pretty ones or solid ones, but ours always seemed to outshine the sun and scream our lively heritage. There was no blending in for the Caryofyllis clan. After Dad positioned the umbrella, he would walk down the beach a short distance and essentially make a flag out of an equally brilliantly colored beach towel and a pole, standing it up in the sand. There was no mistaking Dad's handiwork, even from way out in the water. But that was the point. Before he let us run into the surf, he would make us huddle up and listen to his instructions.

To this day, I can still hear him telling me, "The undertow is really strong today, so when you're out there in the water, I need you to look up every now and again and check your markers. There's the umbrella, and there's the towel. Make sure you're between the two of them. If you find yourself outside the markers, make your way to shore and walk back. If you look up every now and again and check your markers, you'll be fine."

My dad knew how easy it was to drift. He also knew there was an even greater danger if we did.

No matter how good a swimmer each of us kids was, no matter how confident, how strong, how knowledgeable we were of the sea and her currents, if we drifted too far, then drowning was the real threat.

As the old saying goes, "It's the strong swimmers who drown." Dad understood the meaning of this saying all too well: those you think would never drown, could never drown, are the least likely to drown, are actually the ones who do. Those who think they are impervious to the power of the water and take the risky chances that a novice never would are more likely to perish. And once they start drowning, they are just like everyone else, helpless to survive. Despite how fit they may be, they have no control over their actions. They cannot stop drowning or perform voluntary movements like waving for help, moving toward a rescuer, or reaching out for a life ring. Because of that, drowning is almost always deceptively quiet.[1]

Just like drifting. Dad knew one could lead to the other, so he first did all he could to keep us from drifting.

So did the writer of Hebrews.

Pay attention.

Lest you drift.

The writer was speaking to all of us, knowing that any of us at any stage of life could find ourselves in a place we never intended to be.

When we begin to drift in any area of our lives, it's subtle. Hardly even noticeable. Barely detectable. It's not a deliberate step we take but more like a gradual slip. Perhaps it occurs as we make small concessions or compromises. We don't drift because we aren't strong or haven't walked with Christ for many years. It just happens. But once it does, if we don't look up and check our markers, we will be taken places we never wanted to go— emotionally, physically, relationally, or spiritually. There is no aspect of our lives that is immune from drifting and no single person who is not prone to drift.

THE CURRENT OF OUR TIME

My dad did all he could to prepare us kids. I remember him telling us what to do just in case we got caught up in a current, started swimming toward shore, but grew too tired to keep going: "Float. Save your strength. Don't fight it. And know that I'm watching. I'll find a way to get to you." I believed him. I always knew he would be ready to rescue us, all set to do whatever it took to reach us.

> There is no aspect of our lives that is immune from drifting and no single person who is not prone to drift.

Isn't our heavenly Father just as eager to help us when we drift spiritually? He's always watching. Always ready. Always wanting to get us from where we are to where we need to be. That's what the author of Hebrews was inspired to help us grasp. He was writing to the Christians of his day, to believers who had converted from Judaism and were being tempted to drift and go back to their old belief system. The current of their time was pulling them away from the truth of the gospel. Rome had been burned, and the emperor, Nero, was ruthless, deflecting blame from himself to the Christians. Because of his accusations, Christians were experiencing persecution, pressure, and insurmountable problems. They were losing their property, being shunned in their communities, and even becoming martyrs. It was a time of great struggle and heartache. How could the early Christians not have been tempted to go back to the seeming safety of temple worship? There they would be accepted and not marginalized. They would be comfortable and not ostracized. They wouldn't be attacked just for being Christian.

Doesn't that sound like the day and age we're living in? Where everything is chaotic, volatile, and unpredictable? Where everything that once was certain seems so uncertain? Where everything that can be shaken is being shaken? From politics and government to morality and normality to values and beliefs to right and wrong to truth and facts—everything seems to be shifting. We try so hard to be loving and gracious, inclusive and not exclusive, kind and gentle, while still being absolutely obedient to the truth of the Word of God, but it's not easy. It's not easy to stand out. It would be so much more comfortable to fit in.

No wonder the writer of Hebrews kicked off his message in chapter 1 saying,

> For to which of the angels did [God] ever say,
>> You are my Son;
>> today I have become your Father,
> or again,
>> I will be his Father,
>> and he will be my Son?
> Again, when he brings his firstborn into the world, he says,
>> And let all God's angels worship him.
> And about the angels he says:
>> He makes his angels winds,
>> and his servants a fiery flame,
> but to the Son:
>> Your throne, God,
>> is forever and ever,
>> and the scepter of your kingdom
>> is a scepter of justice.
>> You have loved righteousness

and hated lawlessness;
this is why God, your God,
has anointed you with the oil of joy
beyond your companions. (vv. 5–9)

What was the writer's point? What was his focus? What was his emphasis? The unchallenged, uncontested, unequivocal, utter supremacy of Jesus. Jesus, who is greater than all the angels. Greater than all of creation. Greater than any enemy. Greater, I dare say, than even the times in which we live.

Then, in chapter 2, the writer urged the early Christians to keep going, despite the temptation to give up and give in: "Therefore we must pay much closer attention to what we have heard, lest we drift away from it. . . . How shall we escape if we neglect such a great salvation?" (vv. 1, 3 ESV).

It's easy for us to keep going to church, keep attending Bible studies, keep leading small groups, keep worshipping and praying, keep declaring by faith . . . and be drifting at the same time. Don't forget: the writer of Hebrews was talking to followers of Jesus. To people like you and me. He knew that we can be neglecting one thing simply because we're paying attention to something else. That, by all accounts, we can look like we're moving forward but actually be drifting.

- We can be diligently working on our education—and be drifting.
- We can be climbing the corporate ladder—and be drifting.
- We can be starting a business—and be drifting.
- We can be raising strong kids—and be drifting.

- We can be building a cause-worthy nongovernmental organization—and be drifting.
- We can be saving lives in a hospital—and be drifting.
- We can be attending our church, faithfully, for decades—and be drifting.
- We can be serving in ministry—and be drifting.
- We can be reaching multitudes for Christ—and still be drifting.

When I found myself unsure if I wanted to keep going, I hadn't let go of anything. I was still reading my Bible and praying every day. I was still reading great books, attending conferences, listening to podcasts, memorizing verses of Scripture. I was still talking out ideas, plans, and thoughts with Nick, with trusted Christian friends and well-respected leaders. I was even enrolled in a master's degree program for evangelism and leadership with twenty other women. I wasn't going it alone. And yet, I was drifting. Somehow. Somewhere.

Here's what I came to understand: We can be doing all the right Christian things, saying all the right Christian words, but just like the followers in Hebrews, we can be adrift and drifting still further. Maybe because . . .

- We've been disappointed or disillusioned more times than we can count.
- We've been betrayed, and our hearts remain broken.
- We've suffered setback after setback and lack the strength to stand again.
- We've been skipped over too many times and feel left out and left behind.

- We've been punched in the gut so hard we just can't catch our next breath.
- We've failed in some way and fear it is final.
- We've simply run out of energy, vision, passion, or motivation.
- We've forgotten why we started in the first place.
- We've gotten distracted or succumbed to other attractions.

It's easy to drift. It's even easier than we think to quit believing God in the midst of all our believing. To keep declaring doctrinal truths while allowing deadly disbelief to take residence in our hearts, leading us to a place where we are unsure about the future. Unwilling to embrace it. Unable to move forward.

LET'S KEEP GOING TOGETHER

If you had told me a few years ago that one day soon I'd find myself in a place where I wasn't sure I wanted to keep going, I wouldn't have been able to comprehend how that could be possible. I have worked hard for years to be strong spiritually, mentally, and physically. But what I realized recently is that sometimes life happens faster than we can run our race. We can't control everything that happens to us or around us. We can't control the decisions others make that deeply affect us. Even if we've walked with Christ for years and allowed him to do a deep healing work inside of us, we can still find ourselves in a place we never dreamed. A place we never intended to be. A place of wanting to ring the bell.

If that's where you are in any area of your life, then I have good news for you. You are not in Navy SEAL training. This is not Hell Week. This is the kingdom of God, where grace and truth abound (Rom. 5:20). Where his mercies are new every morning (Lam. 3:22–23). Where there is always a way forward.

You are not a failure for feeling like you want to ring the bell. God loves you. God is for you. And he is working all things together for your good and his glory (Rom. 8:28). He has a hope and a plan for your future (Jer. 29:11). You don't have to perform for his love and acceptance (Rom. 3:24–26). Best of all, you alone don't have to figure out how to get out of the place you've drifted to. Since I've been there, I want to help you.

When I was tempted to stop being all in, God never left me. He just kept directing me. Helping me. Strengthening me, so I wouldn't ring that bell. What he showed me is what enabled me to stop drifting and start thriving again. What he showed me is what enabled me to keep going and keep growing. To stay on point, fulfilling all the purpose he's placed inside of me, pursuing all he's called me to do. I haven't discovered all the answers, but looking back and seeing how God moved me forward, I've done my best to capture the insights and understanding he has given me so I can pass them on to you.

Though I learned that paying attention was the antidote to my drifting, what I found even more important was to discover *what* exactly we pay attention to and *how* we pay attention to it, so we don't ever lose sight of it again. That and so much more are what I can't wait to share with you throughout the pages of this book. Through stories from my own life and the lives of friends I cherish, I will show you what I have discovered about the places where we all walk from time to time and the place where I'm walking now.

It's a new place, a peaceful place. One that includes staying on mission and launching the next adventure. One where I sleep better than ever, no matter where I lay my head.

1

DROPPING—AND SETTING—ANCHOR

Nothing is never nothing. It's always something.

—CECELIA AHERN, *THE BOOK OF TOMORROW*

"Chris, drop anchor," Nick shouted to me from the stern of our little boat in the Aegean Sea. We were vacationing for a few days in Santorini, Greece—my favorite place on earth. (Yes, the same place where I've daydreamed about opening a little café.) It was fun to be out on the water and to reminisce about our honeymoon more than two decades before in this same paradise. Just like back then, Nick had rented a boat so we could explore the island and its coves.

Both Nick and I love boating. I especially love the beauty of gliding across the water, watching the sunset, and feeling the salt air on my face. Nick likes more high-octane adventure, and he never minds getting so far out that we encounter shipping lanes where our boat feels like the size of a life raft next to massive cargo ships. (Of course, those kinds of trips just cause me to pray more.)

Today, he just wanted to fish, which meant I could relax. As we left the marina, we headed in search of our favorite small cay and its secluded little lagoon. It was the perfect place to drop anchor.

Whenever we go boating, Nick often fishes while I close my eyes and soak up the sun. Don't get me wrong; I love to fish too . . . as long as I don't have to touch the fish. (Okay, I'll admit it—I'm a total screamer when they come flying into the boat.) The truth is, I like the thought of fishing more than actually fishing, so I suppose you can say sunbathing is my preferred sport.

As Nick set up his gear and cast his line, I went to the bow of the boat and dropped the anchor. Then I stretched out to rest and nap. It was the perfect kind of day. Just the two of us and lots of sun and sea.

I must have dozed off longer than I thought, because when I awoke, the mild breeze had turned into a biting wind. The heat of the sun on my skin had turned into a damp chill, and the boat was rocking way too much for our shallow cove. As I opened my eyes and sat up, I looked around to find us far from where I'd fallen asleep.

How did we get here?

Nick was stowing his gear. "Chris, did you drop the anchor like I told you?"

"Yes, of course," I answered him. (I always do my best to be a great first mate!)

"But did you set it? The current has taken us really far out."

"Did I what? What are you talking about? You asked me to drop the anchor, and I did. You didn't say to do anything else," I said in defense of my expert seamanship.

"Chris, if you don't ensure the anchor is attached to the ocean floor, then we aren't really anchored."

Well, no one told me that part of the equation.

Holding on to the side of the boat, with the waves looming larger and larger, I estimated that we'd drifted more than a mile out to sea—right into the shipping lanes, and this time it wasn't for adventure. Apparently, Nick had taken a break from fishing to nap as well—and neither of us had noticed that we were drifting into dangerous waters, far away from the security of our calm little cove. I looked beyond the nearby ominous ships and saw a storm brewing in the distance, working its way toward us. We'd have to outrun it for sure. None of this was what I had imagined for our day.

As I held on, Nick began to navigate our little boat back in the direction of land. Fighting the current and the waves, he tacked back and forth through the choppy seas and against the fierce wind. I grew nauseated as the boat ran straight up a wave only to fall on top of the next—one right after the other. My knuckles grew white as I gripped the rail tighter and tighter trying to stay put on the seat.

Nick stayed with it. He's always been an expert captain, so I knew we'd make it back somehow, but the journey was nothing less than arduous. It took us so long to reach port that when we idled into the marina, the sun had set and the docks were almost deserted. As we secured the boat in a slip and climbed out, it seemed every muscle in my body that had tensed for hours was letting go all at once. Wobbling toward the car with just a few streetlights and the moon to guide us, I reflected on all we'd just been through—and what had caused it.

Nick had positioned us correctly, facing into the breeze, when he asked me to drop anchor—something he usually managed that I never paid much attention to. If I had just dropped it, held on to the rope, and then given it a good tug as we floated away from it, we would have been secured. The water was so clear, I probably could have seen it take hold if I'd been watching it, but I didn't fully understand the connection between dropping the anchor and anchoring: a dropped anchor gives the appearance of stability, while a set anchor actually grants stability. Only the latter keeps you safe. The other lets you drift into danger, wherever the current is flowing. It will lead you somewhere, anywhere— most likely where you do not want to go. What I learned on the water that day was even more critical than I realized. More relevant than I had ever understood.

It is so easy to drift.

All you have to do is nothing.

THE CURRENT IS ALWAYS MOVING

What Nick and I experienced that day in Santorini was a snapshot of the power of oceanic currents to move us from one location to another. The world's waterways are always on the move. They flow in complex patterns around the globe, affected by many forces—from the typography of the ocean floor to the earth's rotation to atmospheric changes.[1]

Not to give you too much of a science lesson, but from the time I was just a schoolgirl growing up in Sydney, I was taught all about the East Australian Current (EAC) running from the Great Barrier Reef down the coastline of Australia. It's sixty-two miles wide and nearly one mile deep, driven by the South Pacific winds. It flows faster in the summer than in winter. And it is so powerful that it moves entire populations of marine life from one sea to another.[2] If you've seen the movie *Finding Nemo*, featuring the adventures of Dory and Marlin, then you've at least seen the animated version of the EAC, although it's not nearly as fast-moving as Pixar made it out to be. Still, if you get caught in it, then you will drift to where it takes you—whether that is somewhere you want to go or not.

Understanding this and knowing firsthand how easy it is to drift when you're out at sea, I can't help but think about other kinds of currents that are just as powerful and, perhaps, even more dangerous. Ones that involve intangible undercurrents like popular ideas and philosophies that work their way through our culture. And sometimes even into the church. These kinds of influencers are the currents of our time, driven by the winds of change. They take society—and sometimes us along with them— off center, away from the foundational truths of God's Word and into places we never wanted to go. All this happens silently, gradually. It goes on largely unnoticed.

I imagine you are probably more familiar with these currents than you might expect. Just think about how many times you have been forced to grapple with issues you never considered before. Issues that once might never have affected you or your family, but now they do.

Now that my girls are teens, I find myself having conversations with them that my mother never would have dreamed of having with me, but my daughters are facing a world my mother never knew. They are frequently confronted with ideas and perspectives that are much different from the biblical truths Nick and I have taught them. Sometimes these ideas they bring to us are complex and challenging to explain. In those times Nick and I listen, pray, and carefully direct our girls back to the Word of God, doing our best to address both the practical and the spiritual sides of the issues.

Together, over the years, at every age-appropriate level, we have talked about bullying, anxiety, identity, value, and sexuality. We have dissected morality, diversity, and misogyny. We have discussed poverty, prejudice, racism, and inequality. We have articulated everything from apologetics to science. We have covered whatever ground necessary to help Catherine and Sophia see the value of their Christian faith, of their relationship with Jesus and its outworking in every experience they might encounter—especially in the face of the hardest objections to Christianity. And we're still talking. We'll never stop talking. Because the world as we know it—as we have known it—is ever evolving, and it affects us. Oftentimes more deeply than we like to admit.

From our family talks and from what I see happening in the world, I'm all too aware that just as the EAC moves marine life, the currents of our time seem to be moving entire populations of people and how they think and believe to places we might never have expected.

I take comfort in knowing that none of this is a surprise to God. Not the natural disasters. Not the effects of war. Not the fluid shifts in culture. Not the injustices. Not the changes in morality, ethics, or plain common sense. God knew the winds of change would blow through every generation, including ours. And he knew how easy it would be for us to find ourselves drifting—even when we had every intention of never letting it happen.

God knows the frailty of our humanity. He has been

contending with it ever since the fall. He knows how effortless our drifting is. In our thoughts. In our actions. In our day-to-day lives. In the simplest of things. He knows how tempted we are to gradually shift from having our hope in him to having it in other people—a common error that usually works well until someone disappoints us.

It's all too easy to stand on alternate sources of security and significance while saying we are standing on our faith. To put trust in *our* education, *our* plans, or *our* careers. To fall back on what *we* know, on what *we* think has made us successful. To rely on *our* gifts, *our* talents, or *our* abilities—as though we possess them apart from God (2 Cor. 4:7).

> God knows the frailty of our humanity. He has been contending with it ever since the fall. He knows how effortless our drifting is.

And we may be doing all this without even realizing it. Just like I thought I had anchored our boat, sometimes we think we are standing on our faith until we find ourselves somewhere we don't recognize.

For me, now that I know it's possible to drift unaware, that drifting doesn't happen all at once but over time, and that small drifts in our day-to-day actions can produce great shifts, I've built in the practice of taking a personal inventory on a regular basis to prevent myself from drifting again. I am paying closer attention than ever before. To my personal relationship with God. To what's going on in my heart. And where I'm placing my trust. To my family, friends, and colleagues. As Solomon wrote, it's the little foxes that undermine our relationship with God—the things we might not notice, that seem small, invisible, undetected (Song 2:15).

About my relationship with God, I ask:

- Have I stopped pursuing God and started deprioritizing my time with him?
- Have I stopped consuming God's Word and started living off leftovers?
- Have I stopped responding to the Spirit at once and started delaying?
- Have I stopped caring and started growing callous about former convictions?
- Have I stopped praying and started obsessing?
- Have I stopped seeking more of him?

And about my relationships with others, I ask:

- Have I stopped forgiving and started harboring?
- Have I stopped sharing and started withholding?
- Have I stopped committing and started shrinking back?
- Have I stopped laughing and started growing more critical?
- Have I stopped responding with grace and started responding with impatience?

And about my heart, I ask:

- Have I stopped having passion and started having resentment?
- Have I stopped dreaming and started settling?
- Have I stopped hoping and started sinking into despair?
- Have I stopped feeling and started growing numb?

I have discovered—from making this list and digging into God's Word—that there are a multitude of ways to drift, but there is only one way not to. And that is to drop—and set—anchor.

JESUS IS OUR ANCHOR

With so much change in motion, there is only one anchor I know that can hold us steady in such shifting currents. His name is Jesus.

The writer of Hebrews reminded the early Christians that God made Abraham a promise—to bless him and multiply his descendants—and God kept it. Likewise, every generation since has had a promise to hold on to.

> For when God made a promise to Abraham, since he had no one greater to swear by, he swore by himself: I will indeed bless you, and I will greatly multiply you. And so, after waiting patiently, Abraham obtained the promise. For people swear by something greater than themselves, and for them a confirming oath ends every dispute. Because God wanted to show his unchangeable purpose even more clearly to the heirs of the promise, he guaranteed it with an oath, so that through two unchangeable things, in which it is impossible for God to lie, we who have fled for refuge might have strong encouragement to seize the hope set before us. *We have this hope as an anchor for the soul, firm and secure.* It enters the inner sanctuary behind the curtain. Jesus has entered there on our behalf as a forerunner, because he has become a high priest forever according to the order of Melchizedek. (6:13–20, emphasis mine)

God sent us a savior—Jesus, this hope—as the anchor for our souls. But kept inside the boat, inside the grasp of our control, our anchor does us no good. It's only when we drop it outside the boat, ensuring it's embedded beneath the water's surface in the ocean floor, that this hope we have as an anchor for our souls can go to work. We won't know it's working at first, when everything is calm, but when the winds kick up and the waves start to build, we will know Jesus is doing what he promised. If we keep our hope in Jesus, we can stay steady. Immovable. Firmly established. Even in the strongest of currents and the worst of storms. Even when we can't see our anchor in the depths below. "Now in this hope we were saved, but hope that is seen is not hope, because who hopes for what he sees?" (Rom. 8:24).

> God sent us a savior—Jesus, this hope—as the anchor for our souls.

Hope does what it was meant to when we simply trust Jesus and leave our anchor to do his work. Even when we feel the current swirling around us, forcefully wanting to move us, we don't have to give in. Yes, our hope will always be tested—it doesn't change the condition of the sea—but to let go of Jesus, the anchor of our soul, to quit trusting, to become distracted, to lose sight of what's holding us in place, will only set us adrift.

Maybe your spouse has walked away, a friend has cut you off, or a diagnosis has totally blindsided you. Jesus wants to be your anchor.

Maybe you have a child you can't seem to reach. Maybe you've lost your job and your savings are gone. Jesus wants to be your anchor.

Maybe your dreams have been shattered and you feel utterly

lost with no idea what your next step needs to be. Jesus wants to be your anchor.

The writer of Hebrews assured us of this, and later in his writings, he shared that God promised us even more: "Jesus Christ is the same yesterday, today, and forever" (13:8). How reassuring it is to know that Jesus is an anchor who never changes. His love remains the same, his mercy remains the same, his grace remains the same, and his compassion remains the same. Particularly when everything else seems to never remain the same.

What we have to learn how to do is stay anchored in him—especially as the currents of our time grow stronger and stronger.

CHECK YOUR ANCHOR

Every time Nick and I go boating, he does a routine safety check of the boat, ensuring we have plenty of fuel, life jackets, and everything necessary for any kind of maritime emergency. Part of his routine always includes inspecting the anchor and the chain attached to it. I'm always captivated by how he pays such careful attention, checking each link in the chain that connects to the anchor.

Anchors for boats come in multiple designs and are always in proportion to the size and weight of the boat. Simply put, the bigger the boat, the bigger the anchor. Attached to the anchor is the chain. The length of the chain to be used for a particular anchorage is usually five to seven times the depth of the water, and it's dependent on factors like the nature of the body of water's bottom, the present and anticipated weather, the tidal and current conditions, and the state of the boat's readiness, as well as the length of time a boat may need to stay at anchor.[3]

For Nick, carefully studying every link in the chain is how he ensures the entire chain is strong and will hold in the toughest conditions. If he were to find a link that was weak, or one that was broken, he would want to have it replaced immediately with a new, strong link.

Thinking back on our boating mishap in Santorini, even if I had known how to properly anchor the boat, if any one of the links in the chain had been weak or broken and given way, then we still would have found ourselves drifting into those shipping lanes. From these experiences I've learned that, while Jesus is the anchor of our souls, we need strong links in our chain to stay connected to him.

OUR WEAKEST LINK

When I found myself drifting, I hadn't abandoned my relationship with Jesus, but some of the links in my chain connecting us had weakened. Somewhere I had quit taking care of them, inspecting them, and strengthening them when they grew fragile. I had let go of something I had once believed, of something I had once held dear, of something I'll share more about in the next chapter, and the consequences were inescapable—just as they are for all of us.

- If we neglect paying attention to God, then our hearts will drift.
- If we neglect paying attention to our spouse, then we will find ourselves disconnected.
- If we neglect paying attention to our children, then we will experience distance.

- If we neglect paying attention to our friendships, then we will find them strained.
- If we neglect paying attention to our finances, then we will find ourselves in debt.
- If we neglect paying attention to our health, then we will find ourselves sick.
- If we neglect paying attention to our learning and growth, then we will find ourselves stunted.
- If we neglect paying attention to our thoughts, then we will be hostage to untruth.
- If we neglect paying attention to our rest, then we will find ourselves exhausted.

I have heard it said that we are only as strong as our weakest link. Neglecting a weak link can make all the difference in our staying anchored or not. That's why God wants us to check our links . . . so we can stay connected to Jesus. When we find ourselves not where we expected to be, he isn't the one who moved. We are the ones who began to drift. Granted, it's most often unintentionally, but somewhere along the way, we failed to check our anchor, so despite our assurance that we were anchored in Christ—because we gave him our hearts—something gave way.

That's what I want us to explore throughout the rest of this book. I want us to check our most vital links—together— and strengthen the ones that have grown weak. I will talk about links common to us all. Together, we'll see how our links stay strong or grow weak—and the way that can vary depending on our unique life

> When we find ourselves not where we expected to be, he isn't the one who moved.

experiences. We'll also explore how we can grow through those moments. I'm hoping that by opening up and telling you when I failed and when I overcame, when I figured it out and when I fell in a heap on the floor, you can move forward with more wisdom and strength through everything life throws your way.

God has placed each of us here on the earth on purpose and for a purpose. He has plans for us to fulfill in every age and stage of life. But if you're in a place of wanting to ring the bell or wondering how you got here, you might need a little help to keep going. Just like I did.

2

YOU STOP TRUSTING AND YOU START CONTROLLING

[The Christian] believes [God] to be too wise to err and too good to be unkind; he trusts him where he cannot trace him, looks up to him in the darkest hour, and believes that all is well.

—CHARLES SPURGEON

Standing in the middle of the grocery store, staring at the empty shelves, I couldn't help but find it all so surreal. Having walked up and down a few aisles, I stepped to the side and took a break to take it all in. Entire sections of the store had been wiped out completely. There were no dry beans, no rice, no pasta, no cans of soup, no cans of tomatoes. Even the meat case was picked clean.

15

I had heard about the rush on stores, the jokes about stocking up on toilet paper, but seeing it for myself was something else altogether. People really were stockpiling food and supplies like there would be no tomorrow. I understood being prepared for an earthquake and having emergency supplies—after all, we were living in Southern California—but this was something I'd never seen in my entire lifetime. And I knew, deep down, there was more going on than just emptying store shelves. People were genuinely afraid.

About that time, a woman much older than me meandered down the aisle, pausing in front of me, obviously searching for something. "Olives, just one small jar . . ." she mused to herself. Glancing past her at the shelves where the cans and jars of olives normally were, I realized that I had taken the last jar, though it wasn't small at all.

"Here." I laughed to lighten myself and her wrinkled brow. "Take mine. It's not a small jar, but I think it was the last one. Besides, you'll have enough olives until this is all over!"

"Oh, dear, you keep it."

"No, I insist. I'm Greek, and I know the importance of a good olive! Especially in challenging times."

When she laughed with me, for a split second, everything falling apart in the world wasn't. We were just two women in a grocery store, helping each other out and coming together over the love of food. Not two women foraging for ingredients in a time of consumer panic and global crisis.

"Thank you," she said. "You stay well."

"I will. And you do the same."

Watching her stroll away, I thought of how, in the past couple of weeks, my life, and everyone else's lives, had completely changed. The entire world had gone from what felt like normal to being totally upended. COVID-19, a new coronavirus, had exploded into a global pandemic. Now, the domino effect happening all around the world was picking up momentum. Faster than we realized. Faster than we could react to. Faster than governments could create preventative plans. My standing in a half-empty grocery store was just one of many indicators that we were in a rapidly changing world—and we'd have to find ways to adapt.

Making my way to the checkout, I got in a line. A very long line. One that extended all the way into an aisle, as though everyone were ramping up for Thanksgiving or some other holiday. If only that were the case. As patient customers began making small talk, ahead of me and behind me, I listened. Talking to one another, talking to no one in particular, at times even talking in hushed tones—they said it all. Their anxious thoughts. Their worried concerns. Their doomsday forecasts. It was obvious that what had spread faster than any virus ever could was fear—and all that fear brings. Worry. Doubt. Anxiety. Panic. Dread. Even stockpiling.

FEAR WANTED TO CONTROL ME

Driving home from the store that day, I couldn't help but think of the people whose conversations I'd overheard. The woman whose son and daughter-in-law lived in one of the hardest-hit cities—and couldn't leave. The woman whose husband was on oxygen and was especially vulnerable. The woman who was juggling working from home and schooling her three kids, something she'd never done before. The man of few words, still in his scrubs, holding just a handful of items. He probably understood more than the rest of us. Maybe that's why he had so little to say.

Trying to ignore how empty the streets were, and wanting to jar myself out of such worries, I turned on the news. I had made up my mind days ago that I wanted to be informed, not overwhelmed, but it was already growing harder to be one without the other. Just as I tuned in, the network broke to a live news announcement. The shelter-in-place order that the media had been speculating about had just been issued by the governor. It would start at midnight.

Turning into our neighborhood, my growing concerns landed on our girls, and my heart began to pound a little faster. *How will this affect them? What if this scars them? What if all they remember is the pain and suffering? At such a pivotal time in their lives?* Suddenly, just like all those people in line at the grocery store, I had my own reasons to be afraid. To be anxious. To be consumed. To drift in a way that I hadn't in a long time.

Deep down, I knew I couldn't go into the house in such a state. I had to stop and rein it all in. For Nick. For the girls. For my own peace of mind. I had to anchor myself in Jesus, the only one who could keep me from drifting. So, doing what I had done a thousand times before, and probably would do that many times again, I put my hand to my forehead, and I started talking to myself: "Christine, God has not given you a spirit of fear but of love, power, and a sound mind. You might not understand what is happening, but the one thing you know is that God has never failed you before, and he is not about to start now, so you know you can trust him now."

I understand you might think this is a strange ritual, but it is a practice I have developed over the years. When I have a decision to make. When I need answers in a tough situation. When my thoughts begin to spiral, my heart starts to race, and my palms go damp. When everything feels out of my control, and fear wants to take complete control.

THE WHAT-IF ROAD

Little did I know that day how bad things were going to get before they ever got better, but I went into the house securely anchored, calm and ready to be a strength to Nick and my girls—only because I put my trust in God . . . something that has never come easy to me. Something that I know doesn't come easy to a lot of us because trusting God takes intentionality and perpetual, repeated choosing. It isn't passive but active—and our trust is tested with time and trials.

We tend to think that we are trusting in him and that trusting is easy *until* . . . until we start to lose control of the things we've worked so hard to control—whether it's our children, our marriages, our homes, our schedules, our routines, our friendships, our education, our careers,

> Trusting God takes intentionality and perpetual, repeated choosing. It isn't passive, but active.

our savings, or even our spiritual lives, as strange as that may sound. We think we've reached a certain level of maturity, but if we face a crisis bigger than or different from anything we've ever faced before, we realize we have more room to grow. More room to trust.

The pandemic was certainly something like that for me. And

not just because of my concern for my own family. With nineteen offices around the globe for A21, including the one in California that's home to our Propel team, we have always worked with remote team members, but never with every single one of them—and all our volunteers—working out of their own homes. At the time, that was more than two hundred people, and, in addition to them, we had more than a hundred people in our care who had been rescued from human trafficking. Together, with our country managers, we made it work, but early on, as we were adapting to so many changes on a daily basis—and sometimes on an hourly basis—my mind wanted to go down the what-if road. You know the one. It's a fork in the road that none of us want to take, but when it starts talking, it tries to convince us to go left when we really want to go right. It happens with every decision. With every challenge. With every setback. With every crisis we never saw coming.

Over the years, I've learned that one of the signs I might be walking away from trust and moving over into fear is when all the what-if questions start coming—just as they did that day in the car. Each time, I know I can run with them and start drifting or stop them by dropping—and setting—anchor and trusting God once more. I feel sure you know exactly what I'm talking about . . . when our minds just go there.

- *What if* I lose my job?
- *What if* there really is something seriously wrong with my body?
- *What if* I never marry?
- *What if* I don't get to finish school?
- *What if* I don't get into the college I want?

- *What if* I can't pay for school?
- *What if* we get a divorce?
- *What if* the kids start fighting—again?
- *What if* my kid gets into trouble?
- *What if* the car breaks down?
- *What if* the plane falls out of the sky?
- *What if* someone breaks into the house?
- *What if* the market keeps falling?
- *What if* we lose all that we've worked so hard for?

What if... what if... what if...?

When our thinking starts to be irrational, when our thoughts start dragging us down a road where we never wanted to go, when we feel helpless to stop the unraveling that ensues, we're not trusting God in the present moment because, in our heads, we're playing out a future moment. And if we're not careful, we can go from peace to panic, from wonder to worry, from stewarding to squandering, from preparation to winging it, from trust to terrified in mere minutes. It's so easy, when the what-ifs start, to drift not only in our thinking but in everything our thinking affects— our decision-making, our sound judgment, our responses, our beliefs, our emotions, our perspectives. Even our physical bodies.

Our hearts can race. Our palms can sweat. A knot can grow in our stomachs. Sometimes this what-if drifting just feels like a nervousness we can't shake. A mind that won't recall things fast enough. A nerve that won't stop twitching. A tightness in our necks or backs that won't relax. Thoughts that won't let us quit fretting over our health or bills we can't pay—or something even more paralyzing. If you've ever had anxious thoughts grow so big on the inside of you that you had a panic attack, or if you're

21

given to having them regularly, then you know how easily your body can shift from calm into helpless and from tranquil into terrified.

I've experienced this kind of helplessness before, in that season when I wanted to ring the bell. I had given up and gotten up after one of those nights I told you about, where I couldn't sleep, and I went out onto our bedroom balcony to get a breath of fresh air. But instead of relaxing and staying in a place of trusting God, I started ruminating again—and reliving the past only led me to thinking of all the what-ifs. Before I knew it, I was drifting, and my heart was racing so fast I couldn't catch it.

Soon, my body started shaking from head to toe. And I couldn't stop it. No matter how hard I tried. No matter how much I concentrated—or tried to concentrate. It was no use. It was as though my body had grown a mind of its own. I wanted it to do one thing, but it had decided to do another. When I called out for Nick, my teeth were chattering as though I were freezing, and my voice sounded barely above a whisper to my ears. Still, he was there in a flash, and he held on to me until I stopped shaking. To this day I'm not sure how long that was, but I do remember his voice. And what he said. Over and over. "I got you."

Isn't that what God is always saying to us? In one way or another? He's promised us, "I will never leave you nor forsake you" (Heb. 13:5 ESV; see also Deut. 31:6), and God keeps his promises (Heb. 10:23). Still, why is it sometimes easier to give in to our what-ifs than to lean into him? He even promises to keep us in perfect peace if we'll just trust him and keep our minds steadfastly fixed on him (Isa. 26:3). And yet, our tendency is to drift.

TRUST IS THE MASTER LINK

To keep ourselves from drifting, there are times we need to hit the reset button and make sure we are trusting God more than anything and anyone else, including ourselves. We need to be checking the links in our chain connecting us to Jesus, the anchor of our soul, on a regular basis so we don't find ourselves drifting unaware. Then, when a crisis of any kind hits, be it a financial one, a relational one, an emotional one, a spiritual one, a career one, a health scare, or even a global pandemic, we aren't trying to drop anchor in a storm, when all the waves are so high that they are about to overtake us. We aren't scrambling and playing catch-up on trusting God with all our hearts.

Think of it this way: on a typical bicycle chain, there is a single removable link. It's called the master link, though sometimes it is called a quick link or Powerlink. It's what holds the rest of the chain in place. If you want to remove the chain, you first disconnect the master link.[1] Spiritually, this is what trust is in our lives. It's the master link. If we don't trust God with all our hearts and instead rely on our own understanding, then we're more likely to drift in some area. But if our master link is intact—if we're trusting God and God alone—it makes all our other links stay in place. It makes it easier to stay connected to God in all the ways he wants us to be connected to him.

> We need to be checking the links in our chain connecting us to Jesus, the anchor of our soul, on a regular basis so we don't find ourselves drifting unaware.

For me, to fully trust God is to place all my confidence in

him—and everything about him. In fact, one Bible dictionary defines our trust as "a reliance or resting of the mind on the integrity, veracity, justice, friendship or other sound principle of another person."[2] So when I start spinning with all the what-ifs, or I start questioning God and his goodness, then I'm no longer trusting him. Maybe when we find ourselves drifting like this, in order to stop, we need to reframe all the questions racing through our minds, especially the ones that begin with *what if*. Maybe we need to drop anchor by asking one pivotal question: What kind of God do I believe in?

Did you feel the shift in perspective? Ultimately, placing our trust in God is a choice. There are times we trust God because of what we can see, but there are also times when we have to trust God in spite of what we see. When we have to choose to listen to the words of Proverbs 3:5 and "trust in the LORD with all your heart, and do not rely on your own understanding." I believe in a God who is good, who does good, and who is working all things together for my good, no matter what is falling apart around me (Ps. 119:68; Rom. 8:28). I trust in the character of God. The nature of God. No matter if I'm temporarily falling apart inside, and the world is falling apart around me. Nothing changes who he is (Mal. 3:6; Heb. 13:8). Not small problems. Not medium-sized problems. Not even pandemic-sized problems. I believe there are times when, in order to stop drifting, we need to go back to what we know to be true about God.

- God is good (Ps. 119:68).
- God is holy (1 Peter 1:16).
- God is love, and his love endures forever (1 John 4:7–8; Ps. 136).
- God is for us (Rom. 8:31).
- God sings over us and rejoices over us (Zeph. 3:14–17).

- God is faithful to us—and he keeps all his promises to us (Heb. 10:23).
- God fights for us (2 Chron. 20:15).
- God is just (Ps. 50:6; 1 John 1:9).
- God is merciful and compassionate toward us (Ps. 86:15).
- God is always kind and ready to forgive us (Ps. 86:5).
- God knows all things (Ps. 139).
- God does not make mistakes (Ps. 18:30).
- God is on the throne (Heb. 8:1).
- God is in control (Isa. 14:24).

And on I could go. After more than thirty years of following Jesus, there is much I still don't understand, but God's ways are not my ways, and his thoughts are not my thoughts. In fact, the Bible says they are both higher (Isa. 55:9). So my starting point in wading through any confusion I might have is that God is God, and I am not. If I do not understand something God is doing, it does not suggest a problem with God. It just means I don't get it. At least, not at the moment. We rarely have the whole picture all at once. It's as if we're holding a piece of a jigsaw puzzle, and God is holding the other 999 pieces that we don't even know exist yet. We can't see all that he is doing. But just because we can't see all these things—just because we can't trace God—doesn't mean we shouldn't trust God and should instead believe that he isn't working.

TRUSTING GOD VS. CONTROLLING OUR WORLD

We all have ways the what-ifs impact us—physically, mentally, emotionally, relationally, and spiritually—and start us drifting.

25

For me, one of the biggest ways I know I'm about to drift is when I want to overtly take control of something. It's like my own personal litmus test. Of course, we never think we're trying to control until we can't control the very thing we want to control.

I don't purpose to be this way, but I've always been the kind of person who is more likely to take matters into my own hands than to trust God. It shows up in my life when I focus too much on people acting in predictable ways, on liking things done a certain way and everything being in its place. Without meaning to, I can get obsessed with schedules and plans. I guess you could say, without Jesus, I can be a bit of a control freak, but to be honest, it's not entirely without reason. After years of doing the hard work of learning to trust God through every unknown—to embrace the pain of healing and recovery time and time again—I have come to understand that some of my control tendencies have their origin in coping mechanisms, ones I developed having come from a background of sexual abuse.

Still, God invites me to trust him. What about you? Do you tend to start controlling when you'd really rather be trusting God? It can creep into our lives in so many subtle ways. For example, did you know that caring too much about what people think of us can be a sign of control? As much as we'd like to, we can't control what people think of us, and yet we still try. There have been times when I have cared too much about what people thought, and I've had to let it all go and trust God more.

Another way we can start controlling is when we shift our trust from God to leaning into our own abilities, talents, or gifts. God has generously graced each one of us with such attributes to serve him and to serve others, but it's so like us to put our trust in those attributes and then expect the kind of results that only God can give. Control can be so sneaky. How many times have we found ourselves disappointed, disillusioned, or heartbroken because something didn't turn out the way we expected? All because we thought, on some level, that we could control every aspect of a project or a dream, as well as the outcome. No doubt, there are times when we have to give up what we imagine something should look like and trade it for God's bigger picture—to trust that while we might know a certain direction is God's will, how all the details play out are really up to him.

I have found that we can be working on a team, doing our best to work together as a team, and still be trying to control—like when we forget to foster cooperation and begin to demand compliance.[3] We can start controlling in our friendships and stirring up drama, but when we do, we quit being the kind of safe place we want to be. What about in our parenting? It's so important to love our children unconditionally and freely express that love to them—without valuing what they do over who they are.[4] Still, it's easy to slip into pressuring them to perform. Even in our marriages, we can start controlling and manipulating—by giving the silent treatment or dishing out passive-aggressive comments, attempting to guilt-trip our spouse into doing something for us.[5] No matter which of our relationships we're more likely to try and control, it never works.

What we have to accept is that everyone will disappoint us eventually, especially if we're expecting from them what only God can give us, and that's okay. We need to let our bosses, co-workers, spouses, children, and friends off the hook. I've said it many times to Nick, but primarily so I can hear it for myself: "You are not God." It's not an insult to him but a reminder to me that no one can give us what only God can give us. It's my way of taking the pressure off.

At some point, we have to surrender our attempts to control everything and everyone and learn how to place all our trust in God. Still, I understand there are times when it's easier to make like Carrie Underwood and sing "Jesus, Take the Wheel" instead of really letting go and giving him full control. I'm so grateful God never gives up on us. No matter how many times we take matters into our own hands.

EVEN-IF FAITH

I have found that when we live in the realm of what-ifs, thinking about what could happen and then working to control all we can, we're trying to live in the future and not the present. We're giving in to our fears and being future focused.

At the same time, if we're living by faith, which all Christians endeavor to do, then we're also being future focused. How many times have we heard our pastors challenge us to take a step of faith? Dare us to pray and trust God for an answer? Doesn't that make our minds and our hearts shift to the future? Doesn't it make us become expectant? Isn't that what it is to have faith? Yes, of course. "Faith is the substance of things hoped for, the evidence of things not seen" (Heb. 11:1 NKJV). But what do we do while we're waiting on what our faith is hoping for? What kind of faith do we work with in the meantime? How do we trust God in the present while we're going through whatever uncontrollable thing it is we're going through?

Both fear and faith can make us future focused, but there

is a kind of faith God wants us walking in all the time—and *at the same time* as our future-focused faith. It's found in the book of Daniel, when King Nebuchadnezzar wanted to punish three young Hebrew men for not bowing down and worshipping a golden statue he had commissioned. Unlike so many of the children of Israel living in captivity at the time, Shadrach, Meshach, and Abednego knew how to trust God with all their hearts, but because they disobeyed the king's edicts to worship a false god, they were arrested and brought before him.

> Nebuchadnezzar asked them, "Shadrach, Meshach, and Abednego, is it true that you don't serve my gods or worship the gold statue I have set up? Now if you're ready, when you hear the sound of the horn, flute, zither, lyre, harp, drum, and every kind of music, fall down and worship the statue I made. But if you don't worship it, you will immediately be thrown into a furnace of blazing fire—and who is the god who can rescue you from my power?" (3:14–15)

Their response reveals how deeply they trusted God and the kind of faith they had.

> Shadrach, Meshach, and Abednego replied to the king, "Nebuchadnezzar, we don't need to give you an answer to this question. If the God we serve exists, then he can rescue us from the furnace of blazing fire, and he can rescue us from the power of you, the king. *But even if he does not rescue us*, we want you as king to know that we will not serve your gods or worship the gold statue you set up." (vv. 16–18, emphasis mine)

Perhaps you're familiar with the rest of the story. Nebuchadnezzar gave the order to heat the furnace seven times hotter; then he ordered his best soldiers to tie up the three men and throw them into the furnace. The soldiers were burned to death in the process, but the three young men who put their trust in God weren't even singed. When Nebuchadnezzar looked into the fire, he exclaimed, "Look! I see four men, not tied, walking around in the fire unharmed; and the fourth looks like a son of the gods" (v. 25).

It never fails to encourage me when I'm walking through a fiery trial to remember that Jesus was with them in the fire—and Jesus is with me in the fire. He's promised to never leave me or forsake me—and he never does (Deut. 31:6; Heb. 13:5).

To me, the best part of this story will always be their unflinching trust in God and God alone. Not only did they trust that God could rescue them in the fire; they trusted him enough to say, "*Even if* he does not rescue us, we want you as king to know that we will not serve your gods or worship the gold statue you set up."

Even if! That's the kind of faith God wants us to have all the time. Even-if faith is what keeps us tethered when we are in the midst of a crisis, when we do not understand what is going on, when our situation is painful, confusing, demoralizing, disheartening, disappointing. Even-if faith keeps us from drifting. It anchors us. It's *now* faith! It's faith for the present moment and for whatever fiery trial we're going through. Maybe you've learned you can't graduate on time. Maybe you have been given a grim diagnosis. Maybe you've lost a dear friendship. Maybe you have lost your savings or your business. Maybe you've lost someone you loved deeply. And the pain you are feeling is something you've never known and something you never want to feel again. The only kind of faith that will get you through is even-if faith.

God wants us to have both future-focused faith and even-if faith—and he wants us living in the tension of them both. For example, the Bible tells us to look for Jesus' second coming, to keep watch, to be expectant of him splitting the skies (Rev. 6:14–16). But at the same time, how are we supposed to live here on earth in the midst of all the fires we walk through? Because, let's face it, we're always entering a fire, standing in the middle of fire, or coming out of one. Sitting around looking for Jesus to come rescue us isn't going to equip us to walk through the fires, but even-if faith will. Even-if faith looks at life this way:

- *Even if* I get a divorce, yet I will trust God.
- *Even if* I can't finish school right now, yet I will trust God.
- *Even if* the doctor calls and there's something seriously wrong, yet I will trust God.
- *Even if* I lose my job, yet I will trust God.
- *Even if* I don't get married, yet I will trust God.
- *Even if* I can't have children, yet I will trust God.
- *Even if* I lose that friend, yet I will trust God.
- *Even if* I can never quit working, yet I will trust God.
- *Even if* I lose everything I have worked so hard for, yet I will trust God.

Even if . . . Even if . . . Even if . . . That's the level of trust and the kind of faith I want to have in God. Don't you?

- *Even if* God doesn't seem to answer my prayers, yet I will trust him.

- *Even if* God answers my prayers with a no, yet I will trust him.
- *Even if* the answers to my prayers take years, yet I will trust him.
- *Even if* I can't trace the hand of God, yet I will trust him.
- *Even if* . . . yet I will trust him.

THE GIFT OF LAMENT

I don't know who you turn to when you need a listening ear, when you're trying to make sense of something that's happening, and you want to walk in even-if faith, but you are finding it difficult to do. When my mind is racing and I need to get something off my chest, I typically turn to Nick or to one of my dearest friends, as they are the ones who have helped me the most when I've needed to look to Jesus and set my anchor once more. Maybe for you that's your mother, a favorite aunt, or your BFF. For me, what's been especially hard, though, has been the times when what was weighing on me was so deep, so painful, or too hard to understand that I needed more than what Nick or my friends could give me—like when I wanted to ring the bell. In those times, I've needed something more to help me let go of all my what-ifs so I could find my way to having even-if faith. And the something I've discovered is a kind of prayer the Bible refers to as a *lament*.

Though I pray every day, I have found that it's one thing to talk to God and perhaps another when we really get gut-level honest and pour out our hearts to him—when we trust him with the deepest levels of our true selves and tell him everything. Even the hard things. Especially the hard things. It's part of how we get from wherever we are to that place of even-if faith. This kind of honesty—this *lament*—is scattered all throughout the Bible.[6] In fact, one-third of the Psalms are songs or poems of lament. The book of Lamentations is an entire book filled with lamenting. It's five poems expressing anguish at the destruction of Jerusalem in 587 BC.

In the New Testament, Jesus lamented.[7] He travailed over Israel. He wept over Jerusalem (Luke 19:41–44). He spilled tears over Lazarus (John 11:35). Before his arrest and crucifixion, in the garden of Gethsemane, he prayed three times to his heavenly Father, his sweat falling like drops of blood to the ground (Luke 22:44). "If

> I have found that it's one thing to talk to God and perhaps another when we really get gut-level honest and pour out our hearts to him.

it is possible, let this cup pass from me. Yet not as I will, but as you will" (Matt. 26:39). And on the cross he cried out, "My God, my God, why have you forsaken me?" (Matt. 27:46 ESV).

When I think of these passages, I see Jesus demonstrating for us what it is to be honest with our Father, to be surrendered to our Father, to be in a place of faith, willing to move forward, but acknowledging the struggle or the pain, all at the same time. I see Jesus lamenting and giving us permission to lament as well. I see him willing to feel what we feel, willing to lament right along with us when things don't go the way we hope. I see him as human even as he is divine (Isa. 9:6; John 1:1–14; Col. 2:9).

To lament means "to mourn; to grieve; to weep or wail; to express sorrow."[8] Those words alone tell me it probably won't be pretty, and from what I've read in the Bible—in the Psalms and in the accounts of Jesus—I understand that it might even be loud and feel tormenting or come out of us like a "furious rage."[9] It seems we have plenty of permission to cry and scream and just lose it. When I read about lament, it is outward and demonstrative, not quiet and controlled. It comes from a place deep within our souls.

True lament is a form of prayer and surrender. It is a form of worship because it comes *to* God instead of turning *away from* God. So often when we face pain, we go the other way. We distance. Lament doesn't distance. Lament draws near. And as it does, it doesn't accuse God's character but takes refuge in his character. It doesn't say, "God, you aren't good," but "God, I don't understand." It doesn't say, "God, I am turning from you because I don't trust you," but "God, I am turning to you because I do."

Lament is a sacrifice of worship. It's a gateway to deeper trust. It is a declaration, "Yet I will trust you . . . yet I will praise you!" Have you ever been in church, worshipping with all your heart, and poured it all out on the altar and said that to God? I have so many times after I've suffered loss, betrayal, disappointment, failure, heartache, and even sickness. In those times, what has resulted has not been anti-faith or anti-hope—quite the opposite. It has led me to greater faith, greater hope, and greater trust. It's been how I've rediscovered my joy in a time when I didn't have any.

Still, I wonder if we have been led to believe that to be a good and nice Christian, we need to be in control of our emotions all the time, though the Psalms show us that God wants us to pour them all out to him. God is our safe place. He won't be offended if we tell him how we really feel or think because he knows anyway, and it's a sign of trust for us to pour it all out to him.[10] If we don't go to God with it all, then it will seep out as toxicity onto other people or poison us from the inside out—or both.

Before his crucifixion, Jesus said to his disciples, "Truly I tell you, you will weep and mourn, but the world will rejoice. You will become sorrowful, but your sorrow will turn to joy" (John 16:20). In my experience, lament that looks to God doesn't carry us down into a pit but brings us up to a place of greater trust. It makes us recognize our desperate need for God and the bigness of God. It brings us to a place of true humility.

Lament is different from fear or negativity or hopelessness. It's more than just weeping, though in lamenting we do weep. As Christian author and professor N. T. Wright said, "Lament is what happens when people ask, 'Why?' and don't get an answer. It's where we get to when we move beyond our self-centered worry about our sins and failings and look more broadly at the suffering of the world."[11] I have several things in my life about which I have asked God *why*, and after a few years, I still don't understand, and I still don't have answers. To this day, I don't think those situations are fair, and they feel unresolved in my heart. Still, I trust him, but only because I took the time to lament.

I took it all to God, believed he is good, and asked him to fill in the gap between what I believe and how I feel, and he did. I had to get to the place once more where my faith isn't based on getting the answer but on trusting his heart. Can you see how lament is actually a posture of faith and trust because it comes out of a belief that God is good and that God does care? As believers who live by faith, lamenting is how we walk through those in-between spaces where we're waiting and persevering and trusting in spite of all we can't see. It's where we "fight the good fight of the faith" on a deeply personal level (1 Tim. 6:12).

No wonder it's our trust that is challenged the most in everything we face. When we encounter problems of any size that have no human solution, it's so easy to look to heaven and say, "God, why don't you do something about this?" I've said this myself—when I've walked through seriously dark places in countries where I've seen children used to beg, sold as sex slaves, or forced into domestic servitude. It's been hard not to see such injustice and ask God, *Where are you?* We live in a world where there's so much pain, suffering, grief, loss, sickness, corruption, crime, violence, and hatred that it's easy sometimes to get turned around in our hearts and question God and his goodness. But in those moments, isn't it our trust that's being shaken? Isn't that why we start drifting?

With the work of A21, if I didn't know how to lament, I would never be able to sleep at night. But because of lament, I get to give God the burden of it; he can carry what I cannot. I can take all my heartache at the millions of trafficking victims we haven't yet reached and give it to God; then I can rejoice in the dozens that have been recently rescued. My shoulders are not broad enough to handle it any other way, to carry what all is wrong in this world and stay in a place of trusting God. I have to leave it at his feet. And as I do, I recognize and I realize that I am not alone in the suffering. I never have been; I never will be.

When we include the gift of lament in our spiritual lives, we walk in future-focused faith and even-if faith.[12] We walk expectant of the future and fully engaged in the present. Like many theologians, N. T. Wright referred to this as living in "the already and the not yet."[13] That's where our hope rests—in that span of time between what is and what will be.

It helps me to think of it this way: When Jesus came to the earth, he declared the kingdom of God was at hand—meaning he brought it with him—and then he demonstrated it (Mark 1:14–15). He opened blind eyes. He healed deaf ears. He spoke, and those who were crippled walked. He multiplied food. He commanded the forces of evil to go . . . and they went. He even raised the dead. When Jesus came, the kingdom of God broke into the here and now in power.[14]

We know all this to be biblical truth, and we believe that Jesus heals and performs miracles of every kind, even today, but we're equally aware that the fullness of what will be is not here yet—that all as it should be by his design will be in the new heaven and new earth. What that means is that we live in a world, in communities, in families where people do get sick, where relationships fracture, and where pandemics can still sweep the earth. The kingdom of God is already and not yet.

And when we experience the gap between what is and what will be, that's when trust is most needed. When a loved one isn't healed. When our prayer isn't answered the way we hoped, the way we asked. When the floor falls out from under us. When we are waiting. When we are grieving. When we are hurting. When we lack understanding. When what we see—and what we experience around us—flies in the face of what we read in his Word, we need trust. Do we trust him and what he says? Or do we trust in what we see and understand? If our trust in God is limited to our understanding, then we have actually made a god of our understanding and ceased worshipping the true One. If only we would embrace the tension of living in "the already and the not yet," then we could create space for God to be God and for us to grow in even-if faith. Isn't that what we truly want? To trust God more and grow in our faith? I think so.

It's important to remember that no

> When we experience the gap between what is and what will be, that's when trust is most needed.

matter what happens in our lives, our faith pleases God (Heb. 11:6). Both our future-focused faith and our even-if faith. It's what moves us forward. Faith is what transforms us from unbelieving believers into believing believers. From not trusting in the goodness of God to fully trusting in him again—whatever our present circumstances may be. What a gift to have even-if faith!

What freedom to realize that *even if* we feel afraid, we can still trust God. *Even if* we feel insecure, we can still trust God. *Even if* we feel anxiety, we can still trust God. *Even if* we feel completely out of control, we can still trust God. *Even if* we feel disappointed, we can still trust God. *Even if* we feel betrayed, we can still trust God. *Even if* we have made a mistake, we can still trust God. We don't have to drift, *even if* our feelings are trying to, if we stay anchored in Jesus and keep our trust in him.

If we learned anything from the coronavirus in 2020, it was that we couldn't control the future—and what I personally noticed more than anything else was that the people with even-if faith made it through in a completely different way than the ones who spiraled in the what-ifs. Each and every even-if person I spoke to reminded me of the heroes of faith, the ones mentioned in Hebrews 11—Abel, Enoch, Noah, Abraham, Sarah—the ones who the Bible says "all died in faith, although they had not received the things that were promised" (v. 13). Instead, "they saw them from a distance, greeted them, and confessed they were foreigners and temporary residents on the earth" (v. 13).

Like the heroes of faith, let's remember we're just passing through. This isn't our eternal home.

Our citizenship is in heaven, and we eagerly wait for a Savior from there, the Lord Jesus Christ. He will transform the body of our humble condition into the likeness of his glorious body, by the power that enables him to subject everything to himself. (Phil. 3:20–22)

Because we are new creations in Christ Jesus, our legal citizenship is in heaven (2 Cor. 5:17). Our names are enrolled on a register there (Luke 10:20; Phil. 4:3; Rev. 3:5; 13:8; 21:27). We may be residents here, but we are simply sojourners, pilgrims who are just passing through, and as long as we're here on earth, we stay anchored in Jesus by trusting him—and lamenting when we need to so we keep trusting him. That is the way we keep from drifting in the pain, in the disappointment, in the ache of the already and the not yet. It's the primary way we will keep ourselves in a place of even-if faith until the day when we are carried to our eternal home.

And as we do, we set our eyes on the day that is coming. The day written of in Revelation 21:

Then I saw a new heaven and a new earth; for the first heaven and the first earth passed away, and there is no longer any sea. And I saw the holy city, new Jerusalem, coming down out of heaven from God, made ready as a bride adorned for her husband. And I heard a loud voice from the throne, saying, "Behold, the tabernacle of God is among men, and He will dwell among them, and they shall be His people, and God Himself will be among them, and He will wipe away every tear from their eyes; and there will no longer be any death; there will no longer be any mourning, or crying, or pain; the first things have passed away." (vv. 1–4 NASB)

About this day, Jesus has said, "It is done" (v. 6). When Jesus says something is done, it is. It's not that it will be. It is. So lift your head because your future with him—your future in him—is secure. That day is coming. It is sure. It is certain.

3

YOU STOP HEALING AND
YOU START SEEPING

Healing takes courage, and we all have courage, even
if we have to dig a little to find it.

—TORI AMOS

"Nick! What happened?" I half moaned and somewhat screeched
at the same time I took off running to meet him. I had heard the
front door swing wide open and was just about to ask how his
riding adventures had gone when I glanced up and saw the blood
running down his leg, covering the top of his shoe, and leaving a
trail behind him. Being a bit squeamish at the sight of any blood,
it was all I could do not to close my eyes and scream for someone
to call 911. Of course, that wouldn't have been the most rational

thing to do, but who says we have to be rational when someone's bleeding all over the floor? I think I deserved a pass on rational in that moment. Still, somehow, I held it together and reached him before I had time to think of any more unhinged ideas.

Struggling to get under his arm and wrap mine around him, I did my best to bear some of his weight.

"Let's get you to the kitchen and take a look," I said, taking charge, though I would have gladly delegated all my strength had there been anyone else who might have had a stronger stomach. Stumbling our way toward the back of the house, I'm not sure we ever found a steady rhythm, but after a bumpy jaunt, we did manage to get him perched on one of the stools next to the kitchen island.

Grabbing a second stool, I helped him lift his leg onto it, all the while blood was still oozing. Trying to stay calm and kick my brain into a higher gear, I moved around the island, grabbed a clean kitchen towel, dampened it with cold water at the sink, and pitched it to Nick. Even wincing in pain, he was ready for the catch. Racing to the cabinet in our kitchen where all the first-aid supplies and basic meds for kids' fevers or tummy aches are stashed, I surveyed what I had to work with. The Band-Aids were quickly ruled out, as were the anti-itch sprays, aloe gel, and the tablets I had labeled "for a bee sting." We were definitely prepared, if nothing else, for come what may, but I briefly wondered how many bottles and boxes were expired and needed to be thrown out. Never mind. Now was not the time for organizing. (I can totally get carried away ensuring there's a place for everything and everything is in its place. I have been known to throw out everything from dog toys to homework.)

Taking what would be useful, I turned back to the island.

Nick was still pressing the dish towel firmly to the wound to stop the bleeding, though we both knew we had to take a good look and make a decision. Either we were going to be able to bandage this up and tend to it, or we needed to patch it up and hobble our way back out the front door and into the car for a trip to the emergency room.

Letting Nick look first—while I steeled my nerves and determined to be the best nurse I could be—I slowly followed his gaze and focused on accurately assessing the wound. Noticing that the blood flow had already slowed significantly, Nick felt sure the bleeding would stop soon and that we didn't need to rush to the hospital. Nick grew up with a dad who was a doctor, and he'd seen plenty of wounds treated. It was a bad gash, we agreed, but not so deep we couldn't care for it ourselves. It would take some time to heal. But we could manage it, and he would be okay.

How and when he would get back to riding his bike, we weren't sure, but I knew Nick. He would find a way because there was great purpose in his mountain biking adventures.

Nick had just begun to train for one of the world's most athletically challenging mountain bike races: the Cape Epic in South Africa. It's an eight-day race across more than four hundred miles of untamed terrain, with a total vertical ascent of more than fifty thousand feet, depending on the route, which changes every year.[1] He had convinced a team of some great friends to ride with him and raise money for the work of A21.

The Cape Epic is one of those extreme sporting events that is so brutal, people train for years in advance. Well, everyone but Nick. He started one year out, and it was only on his second day riding and jumping the hills near our house that he flew headfirst over the front of his bike. Somewhere on the way to his near perfect landing, he cut his leg—on the bike, a rock, we have no idea. That's when he managed to get himself back home and hobble in the front door.

As we began cleaning up his wound, coating it with antibiotic ointment, and bandaging it, he started telling me how it all happened: "I was doing really great, Chris. Eyes forward where I wanted to go, looking as far ahead as I could see, letting the bike have plenty of freedom to fly over the terrain, just like I'm supposed to. But then, it felt like a jolt out of nowhere. Next thing I know, I've flown over the handlebars and I'm lying in the dirt. It all happened so fast. I knew when I looked down it wasn't going to be pretty. I felt something dig into my leg. I was just glad that nothing was broken."

I was too.

For the next couple of weeks or so, we tended to his wound over and over. Every morning and night we followed the same routine, changing the bandage and checking on his healing progress. We kept a close eye on the wound for any signs of infection. And Nick did his best to take it easy. Though he tried to walk normally, much of the time he limped around or hopped on one foot. He was careful not to put too much weight on that leg, all in hopes it would heal fully and completely rather than burst open.

WHEN WOUNDS FROM THE PAST SEEP INTO OUR PRESENT

When Nick's wound was fully healed, he went back to life as normal. No more hopping around the house. No more reminding the girls to be cautious when hugging him. No more protecting it when he sat down at his desk and carefully avoiding bumping it against the posts underneath. Still, it left a scar. And a tender place. More than once I saw him wince when something bumped it in just the right spot.

Each time, I always seemed to wince too.

Tending to Nick's wound often made me think of how we're wounded in ways no one can see. In ways that don't require stitches or ointments or bandages. That don't require us to run to urgent care for treatment.

I feel sure you know the kind of wounds I mean. They're the ones that have been inflicted on our hearts. That have affected us mentally, emotionally, and spiritually. For a short time or a long time. They're the ones that didn't bleed externally. The kind that no one seems to notice. The ones that might be coming to mind right now. I know I still have a few that I haven't completely forgotten. Not because I don't want to, but because they're the ones that left a tender place just as real as the one on Nick's leg.

I don't know of any way to categorize our wounds, especially the ones no one can see, but some are definitely more easily healed than others—just like physical wounds. After Nick's leg healed, he continued training for the entire next year, and he wrecked his bike a number of times over the months of learning how to be more agile and proficient at mountain biking. Sometimes he got up almost unscathed with just a scratch or two, other times he brushed off a skinned arm or a minor cut, and still other times he added another bruise. But he never suffered another gash like he did that second day of training.

Isn't that just like the nature of our heart wounds?

I think so.

When I reflect on the wounds my heart has endured, I remember the ones that felt like simple scrapes, and the ones

45

that seemed to leave a faint bruise for only a day or two. When I wasn't invited or included. When I was overlooked or dismissed. When I was misunderstood or misrepresented. When someone was careless with their words, leaving me feeling angry or a little less than.

I think of the wounds that went deeper and took me a little longer to quit nursing. Like the times when I felt treated unjustly. When I was called names as a kid just because I was Greek and the daughter of immigrants. When I was treated differently because I was a woman. When someone disqualified me because of my age when I was young, and later when I was older.

I also remember the ones that seemed so painful and so intense, they felt like they would never heal. If you've read any of my books, then you know my story—how I was left unnamed and unwanted in a hospital for two weeks before being adopted by loving parents, but then, as a child, was abused at the hands of several men. For many years. Unable to understand what was happening. Unsure what to say or how to ask for help. Left broken to navigate life as best I could.

Being healed of those wounds from my early life took years of my adult life, and as I wrote in *Unexpected*, it seems there are still residual wounds in my heart that God continues to heal. When my mother died just a few years ago, after years of so much healing, her passing dredged up many strange feelings about my birth mother—a woman I've never known—and God showed me more places in my heart he wanted to tend to. I was shocked. But while some wounds seem to heal quickly and completely within one season of our lives, others heal gradually, little by little, one layer at a time.

Maybe dealing with some kinds of pain all at once would

be more than we could bear. After being healed of so many different kinds wounds in my life—including ones with layers—I have learned to trust God with the timing for each wound's healing. And I've learned that when triggers happen and expose another tender place, we need to invite him in once more. God promises to heal us each and every time—whether it's a wound that

> While some wounds seem to heal quickly and completely within one season of our lives, others heal gradually, little by little, one layer at a time.

heals quickly or in stages—and he always keeps his promises: "He heals the brokenhearted and bandages their wounds" (Ps. 147:3).

For those moments that have surprised me, those triggers that just seemed to pop out of nowhere, I have learned to be thankful because when we aren't healed of our invisible wounds, whether big or small, they invariably seep—and seeping is always a telltale sign that we are drifting. That we have quit going to the Healer for healing. That we have lost sight of pursuing Christ and anchoring ourselves in him the way he intended.

OUR WOUNDS NEED PROPER CARE

Our spiritual wounds—those unbearable aches that we often carry around in our hearts—need just as much care and healing as Nick's physical wound did. Whether they are the result of someone's careless words or thoughtless actions; whether they stem from rejection, betrayal, slander, or abuse; whether they were inflicted by a teacher, mentor, leader, friend, or spouse; whether they seem embedded in our history and target us because of our ancestry, ethnicity, skin color, or something else we simply cannot control—if we don't learn how to tend to our wounds properly so they heal, then they will eventually seep.

Our wounds can seep fear, insecurity, shame, bitterness, frustration, or anger. They can cause us to withhold love, mercy, grace, and forgiveness. They can move us to isolate and lose ourselves. They can drive us to overwork, overthink, or overindulge. They can even lead us to feeling deeply depressed, ready to give up, utterly hopeless.[2]

This is what happened to a friend of mine, Jen, during a time in her life when she was wounded and seeping—and it happened in a way she never expected, in a way that was all too easy. It was early in her career when she was a young professional—fresh out of school, eager to please, and learning her way around office protocols and politics. She had prayed for just the right job, just the right position, where she could shine bright her faith in Jesus. When God gave her the desires of her heart, she was thrilled at the chance to be a light for Christ in the corporate world.

Soon after being hired, she earned the privilege of being part of a marketing team where everyone had to pull their weight in order for all of them to succeed—and everyone did, except for one coworker who always seemed to find a way to do just enough to get by. Just enough to appear as though she had worked as hard as everyone else.

When it came time to promote one of them to team leader, it was "the slacker" who was chosen. Jen's words, not mine. Not knowing how to process such a blow, it was hard for Jen to comprehend how she'd been stepped over for a promotion. She was hurt. Angry. Offended. Disappointed. Resentful. Jen felt it all. She had worked hard, and she wanted the promotion. Badly. She would have understood if anyone else on the team had been chosen. She would have been happy for that person. But not for the slacker. She just couldn't find it within herself.

Jen had prayed for this job, and God had opened the doors. He had blessed her. Which is what made this situation seem all the more unfair. Unjust. That was the assessment Jen couldn't shake. What she had yet to understand was that this was an opportunity to trust God. To trust him with the job and opportunities he'd given her. To trust him with her heart. And her future.

But the more she stewed on it, the more deeply she felt the pain of not being selected. What began as a sting, a scrape, or a bruise slowly grew into the kind of wound that needed tending. In her disappointment, she began to question God, to pull away from him, to trust him less. Maybe not consciously, but deep down she couldn't reconcile why God would let someone she judged as unworthy be promoted before her. But rather than invite God in to heal her broken heart, Jen just tried not to think about the situation. She neglected her heart, and moved on. It was all she knew to do because no one had ever taught her how to process her hurts spiritually, in a way that led to healing.

By the time Jen stepped into her next job, being stepped over had become a wound that was seeping in a way she never imagined. Her skin was a little thicker. Her tongue a little sharper. Her perspectives a little more jaded. Her attitude negative. She became the girl in the office who passed judgment on everything and everyone, who felt it was somehow her responsibility to point out who was wrong and what was wrong, who couldn't seem to find it in herself to celebrate anything everyone else might be celebrating.

Even her social media posts began to reflect her seeping.

Whether it was sharing quotes from others that reflected the same negativity she felt or occasionally even using her own words to cast judgment, Jen's posts served as another platform to air her personal pain.

In our #Instaworthy world, what Jen did was all too common and all too easy. I'm sure most of us have posted something at one time or another under the guise of being "authentic and transparent" when it was really just a smoke screen for venting our frustrations—which were all coming from a place of pain and woundedness. From what I've observed, when that happens, instead of spreading God's goodness in this world, we normally end up adding to the divisiveness and pain inside of us and inside of others. We simply hurt more instead of heal. I know because I've done it myself.

On a few occasions, when I've posted something during a difficult season, close friends who saw my posts and knew it was coming from a place of pain called me. In love, they suggested I take it down, and I did. It's so important to have solid, loyal, and faithful people in our lives who know us and love us enough to protect us from ourselves. I have learned that the number of people God allows me to help is the same number that I can hurt. I understand that what I say and post really matters. I have learned to think and pray long and hard before I post anything, because I want to help people heal. I don't want to aggravate their already painful wounds. Besides that, sometimes we can fool people about our intentions, but we can never fool God. He knows and cares about the heart behind our words as much as the words themselves. After all, he is the one who said, "Out of the abundance of the heart the mouth speaks" (Matt. 12:34 ESV).

All of this was something Jen had yet to understand,

that when we're wounded, we seep, and if we're seeping, then we're drifting—and invariably, we're wounding other people. Somehow. Someway.

Not long after Jen started working at her new job, she read an article in a Christian magazine that opened her eyes. It helped her see herself for what she really was: a wounded person who was seeping and wounding others; a Christian who loved God wholeheartedly but was drifting. It was then that she did the only thing she knew to do, which was the best first step any of us could ever take: she asked the Holy Spirit for help.

"I know it sounds crazy," she said, "but until I realized I was hurting, until I asked God to heal me and I worked to uncover how I'd been hurt in the first place, I genuinely thought I was helping. I thought I was handing out wisdom, not snarky remarks. But I was giving bad advice from a place deeply rooted in hurt and in my own insecurities. I gossiped. Analyzed. Criticized. Even accused. That's what gossip really is: accusation. I spewed poison with everything I said. I stirred up trouble in every conversation. I was like a chemical spill splashing on everyone I bumped into."

How insightful. My dear friend Lisa Harper has often said that what we don't deal with in one season will splash over into our next season. How easy this is to do when we leave one friendship for another, one church for another, one dating relationship for another, one marriage for another, even one volunteer position for another. Like Jen, when we're not healed from wounds in our past, they will seep into our present, enabling us to spread toxicity to everyone around us.

Much like Jen, when I was young in my ministry career, I made mistakes too. I was learning to follow leaders as faithfully as possible when I was given a team of my own to lead. I felt immense pressure not to disappoint anyone. I first felt the need to prove myself to my leaders, to be worthy of their trust in me, to execute every task that had been assigned to me with excellence. Then, to my team, I felt the pressure to prove I was worthy to be their leader, to push them in the direction we all needed to go, to ensure we met our goals. And they were so faithful. They worked hard to meet my expectations. But my sincere exuberance to lead well was overrun by my unhealthy desire for acceptance, and I pushed everyone too far. To exhaustion. To frustration. I pushed for impossible standards. I felt nothing was ever enough for myself, and I passed that on to my team.

Over time, I discovered that I was driven to perform for acceptance. I was called, but I was wounded. And my wound seeped everywhere. I leaked toxicity, and it came out in my words, my attitudes, and my responses to people and situations. My actions felt like something I couldn't control, and they spilled out when I least expected it. I reacted badly in various situations— silently, verbally, emotionally.

I had drifted so far from where Jesus wanted me to be and so far from the standard he laid out when he said,

> You know that the rulers of the Gentiles lord it over them, and their great ones exercise authority over them. It shall not be so among you. But whoever would be great among you must be your servant, and whoever would be first among you must be your slave, even as the Son of Man came not to be served but to serve, and to give his life as a ransom for many (Matt. 20:25–28 ESV).

I remember how the pain in my heart became compounded when I finally recognized my mistakes and felt so upset and disappointed in myself. So deflated. Even condemned. I often mistook God being disappointed in me just because I was, or assumed he was mad at me just because I was. But over time, I learned to live in his grace and to rely on the love that is spoken of in 1 John 4:16. Because the beautiful truth, amid all the hurt, is that he loves me—and Jen. And you. He loves us with an everlasting love, with an unfailing kindness (Jer. 31:3).

Over the years of my life, I have since observed that we all often have intrinsic Achilles' heels—those places of weakness that exist in our souls no matter how great our overall strength. I'm so thankful that God exposed my weaknesses and began to heal me in those early days of ministry. I'm so grateful that he continues to reveal to me places of woundedness. I'm definitely not so healed now that I no longer need Jesus. The closer I get to him, the more I realize I have a long way to go in becoming like him. In fact, it's my utter dependence on him that keeps me growing—and keeps me from drifting. It's a beautiful mystery that helps me stay anchored in him.

With each wound God has taught me to forgive more and more—another essential step toward healing. To extend mercy and grace. To become gracious. To those who I didn't think deserved it. To those who most likely would never even ask for forgiveness. He taught me to live the words of the apostle Paul; though, from time to time, I still don't always manage it perfectly: "Let all bitterness, anger and wrath, shouting and slander be removed from you, along with all malice. And *be kind and compassionate to one another, forgiving one another, just as God also forgave you in Christ*" (Eph. 4:31–32, emphasis mine).

He taught Jen too.

To this day, we both have to be careful. Mindful. Paying close attention to the state of our hearts and what comes out of our mouths so that we don't start drifting once again.

HEALING IS A PROCESS

Whatever our wounds, it's important to understand that because wounds don't fester overnight, they rarely heal overnight. Healing takes time. It's a process. Much like it was when Nick and I kept dressing his wound. I know in my own life I have rarely experienced instant healing, but there's a story in the Gospel of Mark that has always encouraged me in the waiting. It's a story about a man who was blind, who was brought to Jesus for help, for healing. The story takes place right on the heels of Jesus asking his disciples if they had eyes but failed to see, if they had ears but failed to hear (8:18). Jesus healed the man, but not instantaneously.

> They came to Bethsaida. They brought a blind man to him and begged him to touch him. He took the blind man by the hand and brought him out of the village. Spitting on his eyes and laying his hands on him, he asked him, "Do you see anything?"
>
> He looked up and said, "I see people—they look like trees walking."
>
> Again Jesus placed his hands on the man's eyes. The man looked intently and his sight was restored and he saw everything clearly. Then he sent him home, saying, "Don't even go into the village." (vv. 22–26)

This story gets me every time. I have a serious aversion to germs. So much so that I keep hand sanitizer within reach at all times—well, almost all times. And the irony that I feel this way and travel globally isn't lost on me. So the idea of spitting in a man's eyes is a bit much for me to think about.

What's even more strange is that after Jesus spit into his eyes, Jesus laid hands on the man and asked, "Do you see anything?" (v. 23).

Why would Jesus ask such a question? Didn't Jesus know if this guy could see or not? Didn't he know if his miracle-working power was on point or not? And how could it not have been? After all, he is God, right? I mean, up to this point in the Bible, miracles had not been a problem.

And yet, he asked.

"Do you see anything?"

When the man answered Jesus, he said that he saw people like trees walking. He wasn't completely healed. The man saw, but not clearly. He saw, but a tad blurry. He saw, but not fully.[3]

Isn't that just like us? Aren't there places in our lives where we are somewhere between blindness and sight? Somewhere between not healed and more healed? Where things are still a bit blurry—and we need to forgive more? Or once again?

And yet, Jesus doesn't leave us there. He monitors our progression. He tends to our wounds. And he invites us to receive more healing.

When I found myself exposed as a young leader who was demanding too much, I could have passed up the opportunity God was extending to me. I could have remained toxic and deflected instead of accepting God's invitation to be healed. I could have blamed someone. Something. Anyone. Anything.

I could have blamed everyone and every event connected with my past: the ones who sexually abused me; the kids at school who bullied me; my adoptive parents for lying to me about my adoption; my family's Greek traditions that prized marriage and devalued the education I wanted to pursue; or all the mistakes I had made. Even the willful ones.

But instead of blaming, I took another risk and asked God to heal me. And true to form, each time, he showed me a place where I needed to let go of another hurt, where I needed to forgive someone and set them free, so I, too, could be free (Gal. 5:1).

Can you imagine the consequences if I had chosen to blame and not forgive—spending my life living as a victim? I imagine that I never would have stepped into youth ministry early on. I never would have met Nick or had our beautiful girls. There would be no A21 to reach the victims of human trafficking, no Propel to encourage women, no teaching on TV, no books like this one. I wouldn't have a journey of vulnerability and victory to write from. I'd be stuck in a place where none of us have ever really wanted to go. A place of blame and shame and guilt and anger and so much more.

I am thankful that even though it has never been easy, every time I have recognized a wound might be seeping, I have asked God for more healing. More wholeness. More understanding. More wisdom. More freedom. Because as I have learned, there's always more.

For me, every time I've moved from one stage of life to the next, from one initiative to the next—every time God has asked me to reach more people—there were wounds I didn't know I had that God wanted to heal. It happened when I got married, when we had children, when we started our own ministry, and as I've grown in ministry through the years. It's happened as people have hurt me, left me, and betrayed me, when I have failed and made mistakes and even inflicted new wounds on others.

Where do you need more healing? Like the man Jesus healed, we can always stand to see a bit more clearly. How important it is, then, for us to look up and look to Jesus, the One who heals us. That's what the writer of Hebrews encouraged the early Christians to do. He told them to fix their eyes on Jesus, the "author and finisher" of their faith (Heb. 12:2 NKJV). When we take our eyes off Jesus, all we can see is the wound that's hurting or the people who inflicted that wound. Then we start seeping—and drifting. But when we look up and look to Jesus, keeping our eyes on him, we begin to heal. We begin to see more clearly. Just like the man Jesus healed.

What touches my heart even more about this man's story is that when Jesus asked him, "Do you see anything?" the man was honest. How easy would it have been to feel intimidated, to feel pressure to perform, to not want to embarrass Jesus or expose himself as some version of a failure? Haven't we all felt pressure to say yes to someone in such a spiritual moment when the truth was no?

Wouldn't it be great if we felt the love and grace and freedom to always be honest—no matter what? I know that's what Jesus wants. I feel sure that's what Jesus wanted the man to be—and he was. The man didn't lie and say yes; he said no. And Jesus laid

> When we take our eyes off Jesus, all we can see is the wound that's hurting or the people who inflicted that wound. Then we start seeping—and drifting. But when we look up and look to Jesus, keeping our eyes on him, we begin to heal.

hands on the man's eyes once again. It seems the man had a role in his being healed too.

What is interesting here is that Jesus healed someone in two stages instead of one. The healing was a progression instead of an instant change. It took honesty on the part of the man for Jesus to keep working in his life. How many times has God healed us internally first before great change occurred in our external lives?

I believe there's something in all of this for us to better understand.

Let's be honest. With God. With each other. And with ourselves. If we've drifted, if we've stopped healing and started seeping, let's throw open wide the door to our wounded hearts and invite Jesus in once more.

KEEP YOUR EYES ON JESUS

When the verses in Mark 8 continue, it seems the disciples' spiritual vision had begun to clear up, just like the blind man's sight. They were now able to see something spiritually they couldn't see before.

> Jesus went out with his disciples to the villages of Caesarea Philippi. And on the road he asked his disciples, "Who do people say that I am?"
>
> They answered him, "John the Baptist; others, Elijah; still others, one of the prophets."
>
> "But you," he asked them, "who do you say that I am?"
>
> Peter answered him, "You are the Messiah." And he strictly warned them to tell no one about him. (vv. 27–30)

They once were blind. Now they could see. They could understand and comprehend and embrace Jesus and who he really was. "You are the Messiah."

Isn't that what healing produces in our lives? Awe of Jesus. Fresh praise. Understanding. Revelation. Sight. Freedom—from the past, from repeating old patterns of behavior. That's what it produced in my life and Jen's life. But our learning and healing and understanding aren't over. We're still works in progress. Aren't we all?

If we were to walk all the way through the rest of Mark's gospel, what we would come to realize is that even though in chapter 8 the disciples recognized Jesus as the Messiah, they still didn't see him as clearly as they would once he became their risen Savior.[4] Their ability to see and understand continued to unfold well into the book of Acts, when they began to do all that Jesus had saved them for and sent them out to do—go and make disciples (Matt. 28:19).

Our journey of seeing more and more clearly—of being healed of past wounds and growing in Christ—is a lifelong pursuit. It's a journey of peeling back the layers that life exposes and being honest—with ourselves and with God—so we can be healed. It's an ongoing process God wants us to be committed to.

When we find ourselves wounded and being touchy or toxic, snappy or impatient, bitter or negative; when we find ourselves in places mentally and emotionally where we never expected to land, asking God, *How did I get here?* let's recognize that we're wounded, and we've drifted. And if we haven't seen it, let's be open to the spouse, trusted friend, or colleague, who is pointing it out. Then, somehow, someway, let's look to Jesus and ask him to heal us. Let's consider reaching out to a good friend who will pray for us. Or, if necessary, seeking out professional Christian counseling. Sometimes we need help, help that is outside of ourselves or our circle of friends. Let's be committed to doing whatever it takes to stop seeping and start healing. Let's forgive who we need to forgive and make right what we can. Let's keep our eyes on Jesus so we stay on track, perfectly positioned to fulfill all the plans and purposes God has for our lives.

4

YOU STOP WONDERING AND YOU START WANDERING

We wonder why we don't have faith; the answer is, faith is confidence in the character of God and if we don't know what kind of God God is, we can't have faith.

—A. W. TOZER, *THE ATTRIBUTES OF GOD VOLUME 2: DEEPER INTO THE FATHER'S HEART*

"Chris, I just don't understand what's happening," Natalie said calmly, though I could hear the sadness in her voice through the phone. "Two of my oldest friends, people I grew up with, people who went through youth group with me, who even went on to Bible school and served faithfully in ministry, are walking away from God. They're literally abandoning their faith. I know from

61

challenges they've faced that they've had a hard few years, but I never saw this coming.

"I always thought they were both stronger Christians than me because I'm the one who wrestled with my faith when we were young. Not them. They were the ones who stood strong when I was going through tough times in college. They were the ones who prayed with me and for me through so many challenges. They were the ones I leaned on. I can't comprehend how someone can go from being on fire for Jesus and leading others to Christ, to 'I don't think I believe in any of this anymore.'"

Listening to my dear friend grieve over her lifelong friends, trying to make sense of it all, desperate to understand what was happening, I couldn't help but feel a familiar ache. In more than thirty years of ministry, I, too, have had friends who walked away. Friends I grew up with spiritually. Friends I treasured and trusted. When I first gave my life to Jesus, there was a whole group of us who started out running our race together, but somewhere along the way, some of them dropped out. I remember each time feeling just like Natalie sounded: surprised, heartbroken, sad, trying to figure how it had happened, asking God how I might have intervened.

"They're questioning everything they've ever believed," Natalie went on. "And to be honest, I've met so many people like this lately. Just the other day, I met a woman who is in her early thirties, like me, and she told me that she *used* to be a Christian. When I asked her why she felt she was no longer a Christian, she told me a story of how she prayed for years that her mom would become a Christian, but when her mother died, she was pretty sure her mom never had embraced Christ. She said that, after lots of introspection, she just knew she couldn't believe in a

God who would send anyone to hell, particularly her mother, and especially after she prayed so hard for her. There were so many things I wanted to say, could have said, but all I could do was feel her pain and turmoil.

"I know in my own life, I've seen and also been through some things that have rocked me to my core and left me confused and disappointed," Natalie added, "but even in my hardest seasons, I can honestly say that I've never really questioned the existence of God or contemplated abandoning my faith and walking away from God. I've certainly questioned his ways at times and struggled deeply with outcomes I did not understand or felt were unfair and unresolved, but how did I manage to hang on to God and not walk away too? I'm still thinking this through, but I guess it's just all so confusing.

Growing up I was so envious of these very same friends when it came to their relationship with God. They easily trusted God through things they did not understand and readily committed the fullness of their entire futures to following the call of God. I, too, wanted to honor God with my life and to grow deeper in my walk with him, but it always seemed like every good faith step on my part brought with it one million new questions and a constant wrestling out in my heart and mind. Needless to say, I definitely know what it's like to wrestle with questions, confusion, and even disillusionment. But time after time, somehow I've always landed in a place of peace, even when I didn't have all the answers. And for some things, I've never gotten the answer. I've been able to continue to trust God when I didn't understand—and, of course, I've asked you a million questions along the way too. I know my friends sought God, too, though, so what happened?"

Setting my purse and keys back down on my desk, still

holding the phone to my ear, I sat down in my chair and leaned in to give my whole heart to Natalie. I knew she was thinking aloud more than anything, trying to sort through all the clues and her own heart.

"I'm so sorry, Natalie," I began. "I know this hurts deeply. You and your friends have always been so close. You've known these girls forever, and you've shared everything with each other. You have all been blessed to have each other through so many seasons. I know this is hard. When things like this happen, it's shocking, especially when it feels like we've been blindsided. When it feels like something we've loved and cherished is being ripped away. I don't have any easy answers. When I've had friends walk away from God, I've felt such loss, such grief, even when we've remained in contact. I've wanted nothing more than to run to them and help them find their way back. My heart has wrenched at the thought of how God feels. I've had to trust God that he loves them more than I ever could. That nothing is too big for him, and that no person is too far for him to reach. When I've prayed for them, I've had to give them to God."

As Natalie and I continued talking, sorting through her feelings, we both tried to understand, though there was no way to know what had gone on in her friends' hearts and minds.

Finally, I spoke what I knew we both needed to anchor our hearts. "Neither of us really knows how or why any of these people drifted, but as we both have learned throughout our lives, the best way not to drift is to stay anchored in Jesus—and when we find that we are drifting in some area, to drop anchor once more. To go deeper into God. And sometimes that involves asking all the hard questions, just like you're doing now, and letting those questions lead us further into him. Still, I'm aware that when some people ask questions, they move in the opposite direction. They move away from him. That's why it's so important to learn how to ask our questions, and then how to manage all the ways God answers, including those times when it feels like he doesn't give us an answer."

THE POWER OF WRESTLING WITH OUR QUESTIONS

There was nothing I wanted to do more that day than to comfort Natalie and help her friends find their way back to Jesus. But I knew Natalie. She would pray for her friends and the woman she'd just met. She would reach out to them. She would listen. She would be there for them. And do all she could. She was the one God had put in their path, not me. Natalie was more than able to help them because she was a woman who had taken the time to wrestle with her own faith, who had learned how to anchor herself in Jesus, and who had learned to keep anchoring herself so she wouldn't drift.

When I first met Natalie, she was a senior in college. I spoke at her church, and afterward I remember her introducing herself to me and telling me what she was studying in school. She told me about her career dreams and where she hoped to work, among other things, but as we got to know each other, what caught my attention the most was her passion for God and insatiable thirst to understand more about him. I had not met a young woman with so many questions about, well, everything.

Though I don't remember Natalie's specific questions from that night, I do remember us talking at length. Naturally, being asked questions about the Bible is pretty much a normal occurrence if you do what I do. Through the years, I have been asked all kinds of things by Bible trivia fans and skeptics alike. One of my all-time trivia favorites is, besides Adam and Eve, who in the Old Testament did not have parents? Answer: Joshua the son of *Nun* (Ex. 33:11). And my favorite from the skeptics who try really, really hard to hold out as long as possible on believing God: "Could God create a rock so heavy he could not lift it?"

Kids are the funniest, of course. They're the ones who ask, "If there were only two rabbits on the ark, how many were there forty days later?" That's when I start looking around for their mothers. I'm not about to get into a discourse on reproduction with middle schoolers.

Without fail, at least once or twice a year someone asks me how I feel about tattoos and if I have one—and if they are biblical or not. Let me just say that I don't like needles, so that makes getting a tattoo difficult for me. And I'm never quite sure why whether I have a tattoo or not is so important.

All jokes aside, what I do remember most about Natalie's questions was recognizing how much she had sought to understand God's Word. Her sincerity moved me. She was hungry to know God better and to grasp the depths of who he is. To be honest, I felt like I was looking at someone who was wrestling as I had when I was her age. Over the following months, I continued to answer her questions. Through emails. Through texts. Through meeting up with her when I spoke in a church or at a conference near her.

She often told me of her close friends—and how many of them felt called to a vocation in ministry—something that tugged at her heart from time to time, though from the age of ten she had set her heart on being a lawyer. As she put it, every time she watched *Matlock* or *Law & Order,* she just knew it was her destiny. Still, the idea of ministry never left her.

By the time she graduated, she was wrestling with her next career move. She felt torn between going to law school and stepping into ministry. Having heard me talk so much about the beauty of Sydney, with its famous opera house, incredible zoo, and sprawling beaches, as well as the stunning Sydney Harbour Bridge, she asked if she could come and serve as an intern for us, taking a gap year of sorts. Our ministry was still based there at the time, and we were thrilled to have her join us while she figured out her future. We have always had interns, and Natalie was one of the early ones, even getting in on the ground floor of researching human trafficking before we launched A21.

While she was with us, she and Annie—who is still a part of our team—went on a scouting trip for us to several Asian-Pacific countries. What they brought back to us became an integral part of the work of A21 in that region years later.

When her year in Sydney came to an end, Natalie had wrestled with so many questions that she was more confident in her faith than ever. She was anchored. She fully trusted God, and she knew what God really wanted her to do. She returned home and prepared to go to law school.

Not long after she started, God began to weave her passion for law with her newfound understanding of the global issue of human trafficking. Reaching out to her fellow students, she started an on-campus, anti–human trafficking group that was hugely successful and continues to make a lasting impact on students, the university, and its community to this day. The first position she acquired after graduation found her working in the governor's office. There she was able to help orchestrate a landmark bill being passed against human trafficking—the first of its kind in her home state. Nick and I even attended the signing, celebrating with Natalie such groundbreaking legislation. Since that time, Natalie has continued to work in her state's government, affecting the rights and well-being of others.

I'm so thankful for Natalie, for who she is and what she's accomplished, but what I cherish most is the friendship we enjoy to this day—and the questions she continues to ask.

ASK ME A QUESTION—ABOUT ANYTHING!

When Natalie called me that day, heartbroken over her friends who were walking away from God, I had just finished meeting with our newest group of interns in the California office—young men and women from around the world who are smart, imaginative, passionate, and bold, most of whom are college age, just like Natalie was when she served as an intern. Meeting them and welcoming them is one of my all-time favorite things to do. I am always so impressed by how full of faith and joy and optimism they are, and how they want to make a difference in this world.

During their time with us, and when I'm in the office, I do my best to answer any questions our interns may have—about anything. Work. Life. The Bible. Spiritual matters. Social justice. Human trafficking. Dating. I'm forever trying to play matchmaker for any of the singles who want to be married. I'm not sure I've ever succeeded at introducing anyone to their future mate, but with the reach of social media, I keep trying. Surely, one day someone will say he first saw his wife on my Insta story! I'll keep you posted.

But seriously, I do all I can to encourage them to ask me questions. I want to hear what's on their minds. I want to hear what concerns them. I want to hear what their struggles are, what their hopes and aspirations are. I want to learn what things they are confronting in culture and in their everyday lives. I have found it so important to be in touch with them because they are navigating a world I didn't have to when I was their age and just starting out in my ministry career.

I do the same thing with my daughters and their friends. So many times, as they've gathered around our kitchen island or when I've been driving them to the movies, I've said to them, "Ask me a question. Any question." It usually starts out like fun and games, and we laugh and joke, but soon it turns to real issues they're facing or something that someone they know is facing. It turns into questions about the Bible and God's perspective about what's going on in our world today. The questions they've asked have given me so much insight into their lives.

I want them all to know that asking questions is more than okay. It's good. For as long as I can remember, I have always been a girl who asks questions. I feel sure my first word must have been "Why?" rather than the typical "Mum-mum" or "Da-da." For some reason, I've never taken anything at face value, and I've always questioned everything. Even in school, I asked question after question. And I'm still that kid. In 2016, I started graduate school at Wheaton College to work on my master's degree in evangelism and leadership. I'm part of a Propel cohort, and I'm confident that I'm still the one who asks the most questions in class.

Asking questions is how we wrestle with our faith and grow. It's one of the ways we keep ourselves from drifting. As Christians, we confidently profess that we believe in God, but if we don't live a life of unpacking what that actually means, by continually asking questions and following that up with searching God's Word for the answers, we'll find ourselves saying we believe in something we might not ever understand. We might even find ourselves putting more faith in our feelings than in God's Word. Putting more trust in what we can explain. In what we can predict and control. We might even find ourselves valuing our questions over finding the answers—especially if we're afraid of the answers. After all, answers have the potential to call us into account and hold us responsible for what they reveal. If we get distracted or sidetracked on our way to finding the answers, it's easier to become untethered from our faith, to find ourselves unanchored and being carried away by the currents of our time, drifting to places we never expected.

Asking questions is not what causes us to drift. If we're facing a crisis, it's not the crisis that causes us to drift. It's what we do with our questions and with the crises that makes a difference. Jesus is the anchor for our souls, and becoming untethered to our anchor, particularly in the quest for answers to our questions, is what sets us adrift.

Jesus wants us to wonder, but not wander. He wants us to wonder—to ask all the questions that come up in our hearts and minds—but not wander away from him as we wonder.

When we have questions, God wants us to seek answers—in his Word, in prayer asking him directly, in Christian Bible studies and books like this one, and in conversations with anchored Christ followers. When I've had questions, at every age and stage of my journey, I have researched the resources available to me. My going back to grad school is a big part of this, too, because there are so many questions to be asked and so many answers to be found. I have talked to trusted friends and leaders. I've gone to women who were more mature than me or further down the road than I was. I want the wisdom that the Bible says is found in many counselors (Prov. 11:14). God wants us having the right conversations with the right people so we land in the right place. Especially when our questions cause us to question God.

In our search for answers, it's important we don't get lost in what the Bible describes as meaningless discourse or fruitless discussions (1 Tim. 1:6). God doesn't want us to get caught up in foolish debates (Titus 3:9). He doesn't want us to find ourselves being pulled away by an undertow of empty philosophies.

> God wants us having the right conversations with the right people so we land in the right place. Especially when our questions cause us to question God.

God wants us to seek out wise Christian counsel, and then to listen to the counsel—even if, and especially when, that counsel says what we find hard to hear. Daring to ask someone who will give us some pushback and who will offer us some course-correcting advice is genuinely pursuing God. If we reject wise counsel, arguing against it, we need to recognize that as a sign we are already drifting. God wants us to find the right voices to speak into our lives. Voices other than the current cultural trends. Voices other than our own. Voices that speak God's truth, not those that offer their own thoughts. Voices that say, "Let's evaluate this by what God has to say." And when those voices speak truth, he wants us to take it to heart.

I understand that as we seek out answers, there will always be situations we can't explain, when we have to walk by faith and not by sight (2 Cor. 5:7). When we will have to trust God with all our hearts and not lean on our own understanding (Prov. 3:5). I have a ton of those situations in my own life. When I've been hurt. When I've been betrayed. When I've been disappointed or disillusioned. When I've failed and things didn't go as I had expected or planned. When people I loved have died way too soon. When storms have come. When sickness has come. In all those times, I've had to keep trusting in the character of God. I have had to embrace the mystery of faith. I've had to accept that, just like Paul wrote to the Corinthians, there will always be things I may never see clearly on this side of eternity, and that as long as I'm on this earth, there will always be things I can only understand partially (1 Cor. 13:9).

In other words, there will always be a lot of questions for which you and I will never have the answers. Still, God wants us to ask our questions. He wants us to dare to believe there's no question too big for him to handle. There's nothing we can ask that will shock him. After all, he's God. And even when we receive the answers, he still wants our faith, our trust, to be in him—not in the answers or in our understanding. Answers help, but they are not our source of hope. He is. When we understand and when we don't.

Jesus modeled the inherent value in asking questions by asking them himself. When he moved to heal someone, he often posed a question. To the man at the pool of Bethesda he asked, "Do you want to be healed?" (John 5:6 ESV). To the two blind men he asked, "What do you want me to do for you?" (Matt. 20:32). To the woman with the issue of blood who touched the hem of his garment, he turned around and asked, "Who touched me?" (Luke 8:45).

When Jesus was teaching, his questions often seemed to

predicate a powerful truth he was about to teach or served as the punch line for one he just taught: "Who of you by being worried can add a single hour to his life?" (Matt. 6:27 NASB). "Why do you look at the speck of sawdust in your brother's eye and pay no attention to the plank in your own eye?" (Matt. 7:3 NIV). "Salt is good, but if it loses its saltiness, how can you make it salty again?" (Mark 9:50 NIV; see also Luke 14:34).

The Bible has more than three thousand questions in all.[1] In addition to the questions Jesus asked, it is full of instances of people bringing questions to God. Inquiring about God's name, Moses asked, "What shall I say to them?" (Ex. 3:13 ESV). In the New Testament, people asked questions like:

- "Why do you speak to them in parables?" (Matt. 13:10 ESV).
- "Lord, how many times shall I forgive my brother or sister who sins against me?" (Matt. 18:21 NIV).
- "Then who can be saved?" (Mark 10:26).
- "What must I do to inherit eternal life?" (Luke 18:18).
- "Are you greater than our father Jacob?" (John 4:12 ESV).
- "Rabbi, who sinned, this man or his parents, that he was born blind?" (John 9:2).

Going to God with our questions is part of how we make our faith our own. It's how we draw near to him and get to know him more. It's how we learn to stay anchored, even when the winds are blowing and the waves are raging. Even when the currents underneath are growing strong. Digging our anchor in deeper and deeper is how we keep ourselves from becoming untethered to our faith, drifting to places we never wanted to go.

WHERE DID YOU DROP ANCHOR?

It can be hard to stay anchored while wrestling with honest questions. It seems that in every generation there are issues that arise out of the shifting currents of the day. Issues that lead to questions we really should wrestle with, but also that can draw us away from God if we're not careful. So while it is important to ask the questions that arise, we should also remember that whatever the big issue of today is, it won't be the big issue of tomorrow, for tomorrow will have new issues. Only Jesus remains the same yesterday, today, and forever. How important, then, to make him our anchor so we won't be pulled away by the issues.

I understand how the struggle to find congruency with science and creation, world history and biblical accounts, mortality and eternal life can feel disconcerting. It's tempting in our quest for truth to give up too quickly and miss what God wants us to discover. And that is not what we should do. Still, no matter how many questions we ask or how much research we conduct, we need to keep our eyes trained on Jesus. In the end, faith is faith. There will always be answers we have to accept that we might not want to hear. And there will always be answers we may never understand—at least not until we're standing on the other side of eternity in the presence of the One who knows everything. In the meantime, we have to ask ourselves, *Can we trust when we do not understand? Can we believe when we do not understand?* And even when we do receive answers, when we grow in our understanding, will we remain committed to trusting in him, having confidence in him, having faith in him . . . viewing the answers as a help, but not as our hope?

I can't help but wonder about Natalie's friends. What issues were they grappling with when they decided to walk away? Did they dig their anchors in something other than God and his Word? Did they get caught up in the culture of Christianity rather than truly knowing Christ? At what point in their journeys did they quit asking questions? The kind that take us further into God instead of away from him?

I have no way of knowing. But I wonder: Maybe they didn't wrestle enough earlier in their walk with Christ. Maybe they didn't ask enough questions. Especially the hard ones. Or maybe they did, and when they heard the answers, they didn't want to accept them. That happens too.

THE MOTIVE OF OUR QUESTIONS

Sometimes when we ask questions, we hear the answers, but we don't want to face them. They seem too hard to incorporate into our lives or our current beliefs. Perhaps we get caught in a place between our own experiences and how God is leading us. I've read the Word of God plenty of times and felt it begin stirring my heart. I've felt nudged by the Holy Spirit as he illuminated truth to me from a passage of Scripture. Each time that has happened, I've become aware of how God has wanted me to grow in my faith or of a change he wanted me to make. Isn't that what happened when God began to speak to me from Hebrews? *Pay attention, lest you drift.*

Each time God has nudged me, I've been aware that I can pay closer attention. I can believe him and lean further into him, or I can ignore his leading. I can categorize his answer as too hard and not do it. I can dig my anchor in deeper or actually begin to hoist it. When we obey God, when we respond to his Spirit's leading, our anchor remains. It actually becomes more secure. But when we disobey, when we ignore or make light of the Spirit's leading, we begin to raise our anchor. And when we do, we'll find ourselves drifting in that area of life.

God wants us to ask questions, and he wants those questions to lead us further into him. When they don't, the reason can sometimes be found by examining the motives of our questions. Are we asking to grow, or not? Are we willing to accept the truth, or not? Are we willing to course-correct in areas where God might reveal to us that we are off, or not?

When I wanted to ring the bell, I was shaken to realize I had drifted. It was scary to find myself in such a place. But God was being merciful to me. He was extending grace to me. By showing me where I wasn't anchored, he was inviting me to go deeper.

There's a story in John 6 that illustrates this so well. It's woven throughout the entire chapter, so I'll summarize the first twenty verses for you. Jesus had been healing the sick, and crowds of people had begun following him. One day, as Jesus and all the people reached a mountainside, there were as many as twenty thousand men, women, and children who had followed him there. Recognizing they were hungry, Jesus performed a miracle and fed them all using a little boy's lunch of two fishes and five loaves. When the people saw the miracle of what he had done, they were captivated by him. They wanted to exalt him, to crown him King Jesus and follow him to Jerusalem to overthrow Rome.

Knowing their intentions, Jesus slipped away. Later that night, as his disciples were crossing the Sea of Galilee in a boat, he walked out onto the water and joined them. The next morning, the crowd on the mountainside found Jesus missing, so they got into their own boats and crossed the Sea of Galilee to Capernaum in search of him (v. 24).

The chapter's remaining verses contain a discourse between Jesus and the people in the synagogue in Capernaum. The people began asking Jesus questions when he arrived. He answered them by saying, "Truly I tell you, you are looking for me, not because you saw the signs, but because you ate the loaves and were filled. Don't work for the food that perishes but for the food that lasts for eternal life, which the Son of Man will give you, because God the Father has set his seal of approval on him" (vv. 26–27).

Then they asked, "What can we do to perform the works of God?" (v. 28).

Jesus replied, "This is the work of God—that you believe in the one he has sent" (v. 29).

Then they pressed further, asking him what sign he was going to perform *so they could believe.* They referenced how God gave the children of Israel manna (bread) to eat in the desert (vv. 30–31).

What I notice thus far in this passage is that they were asking questions, but the tone of their questions didn't sound as though they were eager to learn. Eager to go deeper. Truly wrestling with their faith from a place of humility. Instead, they were asking with suspicion and hostility, which is more than just asking questions. It's doubting. And doubting involves judgment about God's character. Doubting is an accusation rather than a genuine quest for understanding—it doesn't come from a place of trusting in the goodness of God.

Still, Jesus answered them and began to explain how he is the Bread of Life: "Truly I tell you, Moses didn't give you the bread from heaven, but my Father gives you the true bread from heaven.

For the bread of God is the one who comes down from heaven and gives life to the world" (vv. 32–33).

They responded by telling him to give them the bread anyway. Jesus went on:

> I am the bread of life. . . . No one who comes to me will ever be hungry, and no one who believes in me will ever be thirsty again. But as I told you, you've seen me, and yet you do not believe. Everyone the Father gives me will come to me, and the one who comes to me I will never cast out. For I have come down from heaven, not to do my own will, but the will of him who sent me. This is the will of him who sent me: that I should lose none of those he has given me but should raise them up on the last day. For this is the will of my Father: that everyone who sees the Son and believes in him will have eternal life, and I will raise him up on the last day. (vv. 35–40)

At that, the Jews began to complain and find fault with Jesus. Eventually, Jesus told them to quit complaining and said, "Truly I tell you, anyone who believes has eternal life. I am the bread of life. Your ancestors ate the manna in the wilderness, and they died. This is the bread that comes down from heaven so that anyone may eat of it and not die. I am the living bread that came down from heaven. If anyone eats of this bread he will live forever. The bread that I will give for the life of the world is my flesh" (vv. 47–51).

Still, the Jews argued, "How can this man give us his flesh to eat?" (v. 52).

They were totally misunderstanding Jesus, yet Jesus continued speaking.

Truly I tell you, unless you eat the flesh of the Son of Man and drink his blood, you do not have life in yourselves. The one who eats my flesh and drinks my blood has eternal life, and I will raise him up on the last day, because my flesh is true food and my blood is true drink. The one who eats my flesh and drinks my blood remains in me, and I in him. Just as the living Father sent me and I live because of the Father, so the one who feeds on me will live because of me. This is the bread that came down from heaven; it is not like the manna your ancestors ate—and they died. The one who eats this bread will live forever. (vv. 53–58)

Jesus said he was the Bread of Life and that whoever comes to him will never grow hungry. All the people had to do was believe in Jesus, but to their ears, what Jesus said was too hard. His teaching sounded harsh, disturbing, even blasphemous. Eating his flesh and drinking his blood sounded like cannibalistic religion to them—something they understood happened historically. But they were missing the point.

The crowd following Jesus was attracted to Jesus, but with all the wrong motives. They did not recognize him as the Son of God, as the bread of eternal life, but as a miracle worker who could feed them lunch. They were so shortsighted. And their lack of understanding began to expose how untethered to him they were.

They believed in what Jesus could do for them, but not in who he was. Though, by all appearances, they were pursuing him, even following him out to a mountainside and then across the Sea of Galilee, they weren't anchored in the revelation of who he was. They had flawed followership.

At the very beginning of his discourse, Jesus said, "This is the work of God—that you believe in the one he has sent" (v. 29).

Jesus was inviting them to believe in him and allow their lives to be intertwined with him. He wasn't inviting them to obey religious rules and just go through the motions of going to church and reading the Bible, but to be consumed. To believe. To have faith.

Rather than have a change of heart, they rejected his invitation: "Therefore, when many of his disciples heard this, they said, 'This teaching is hard. Who can accept it?'" (v. 60).

Jesus, knowing they were complaining once again, asked, "Does this offend you? Then what if you were to observe the Son of Man ascending to where he was before? The Spirit is the one who gives life. The flesh doesn't help at all. The words that I have spoken to you are spirit and are life. But there are some among you who don't believe. . . . This is why I told you that no one can come to me unless it is granted to him by the Father" (vv. 61–65). The Bible tells us that "from that moment many of his disciples turned back and no longer accompanied him" (v. 66).

Jesus was unfollowed—long before you or I ever were. Long before the advent of social media and virtual friendships. The crowd that had once been obsessed with him, who appeared to want to follow him everywhere, who had wanted to make him King Jesus, walked away.

When they asked questions, and Jesus answered, and that answer involved Jesus making a demand that required more trust and more faith than understanding, the people walked away. They unfollowed Jesus.

When the crowd walked away, Jesus turned to the twelve disciples who were left and asked, "Do you want to go away as well?" (v. 67 ESV).

It was Simon Peter who answered first, "Lord, to whom shall we go? You have the words of eternal life, and we have believed, and have come to know, that you are the Holy One of God" (vv. 68–69 ESV).

I feel as though I can hear Jesus' heart breaking as he asked, "Do you want to go away as well?"

I'm so thankful that Peter made the connection between the words of Jesus and Jesus himself. His answer was remarkable. An act of mighty faith.

"Lord, to whom shall we go?"

Truthful answers to our questions will always be found in Jesus. And if we will let them take us deeper into him, we will always stay anchored in him. But after thirty years, I can assure you—even when I have felt myself stumbling in the dark, devoid of understanding; even when he has healed me of one thing but not of another thing; even when I have cried, desperate for answers only to hear silence—I have never been able to walk away. Even when I've been exhausted, weary, and ready to give up, I could not. Even when I have felt disappointed, disoriented, and destabilized, I could not. Even when I wanted to ring the bell, as badly as I thought I wanted to, I could not.

The words to the old hymn "I Have Decided to Follow Jesus" make this declaration, and they remain the anthem of my soul:

> *I have decided to follow Jesus.*
> *I have decided to follow Jesus.*
> *I have decided to follow Jesus.*
> *No turning back, no turning back.*
> *Though none go with me, still I will follow. . . .*
> *The world behind me, the cross before me. . . .*

No matter what I have faced in my life, when it has come right down to it, I could not unfollow Jesus. Because there is no one like him. There is no other person, belief system, religion, philosophy, or cause that can do what Jesus does.

There is no other Savior.

There is no other Lord.

There is no other anchor for my soul.

I feel as Peter did: "Lord, to whom shall we go?"

I'm well aware that . . .

- If I want my sins forgiven, where else can I go?
- If I want eternal life, where else can I go?
- If I want my guilt removed, where else can I go?
- If I want my burdens lifted, where else can I go?
- If I want to find lasting purpose in life, where else can I go?
- If I want to find hope in life, where else can I go?
- If I want to be fully loved, where else can I go?
- If I want to be fully seen and known, where else can I go?
- If I want freedom, where else can I go?

Nowhere.

I'll never stop asking questions, and when I don't get the answers I hope for, I still would rather have Jesus than answers.

Following God will always require faith, and genuine faith in God cannot walk away. There will always be things we can't figure out, can't understand, and may never know the answers to, but our worst day with Jesus will always be better than our best day without him. Of that I'm sure. Jesus is the prize.

It takes faith to keep following Jesus.

It takes faith to trust when we do not understand.

It takes faith to remain obedient.

It takes faith to live opposite to the world's standards.

It takes faith to deal with disappointment, discouragement, and disillusionment.

It takes faith to navigate the injustice and suffering in our world.

It takes faith to withstand ridicule and accusation.

> There will always be things we can't figure out, can't understand, and may never know the answers to, but our worst day with Jesus will always be better than our best day without him.

It takes faith to get up and keep going when we have failed or made a mistake.

It takes faith to be a witness for Christ.

It takes faith to hold on to the truth that God is good when life is not.

It takes faith to keep following when we don't know where we are going.

It takes faith to keep believing when we are full of unbelief.

It takes faith to stay strong and courageous.

It takes faith to remain loyal.

It takes faith to live on purpose and stay on mission.

It takes faith to wonder and never wander.

It takes faith to stay anchored in Jesus and not drift—to never walk away. No matter what.

Besides, where would we go?

5

YOU STOP PRAYING AND YOU START TALKING

Prayer is as necessary as the air, as the blood in our bodies, as anything to keep us alive—to keep us alive to the grace of God.

—MOTHER TERESA

"I see a man, one of our own, but not. One who's close, but from far away. One with great fortune. He's for you, Christina. He's exactly what you need. And he doesn't seem to mind your age either. That is good for you, no?"

All I could do was turn my head away from my aunt's questioning gaze and roll my eyes. Theía Maria had been seeing me married off in her coffee grounds since I was fifteen. And though my mum and all my aunts were always mesmerized by how seriously she took her grounds, hanging on to every word she uttered, desperate to believe what she saw in the shapes and patterns clinging to the sides of her cup, she'd never gotten one prediction right. I was twenty-six at the time, and as long as I could remember, she had been rolling her cup around, letting the grounds lay out the future.

"Let the coffee talk to you," she would say, always dropping her voice to add an air of mystery. For decades, Theía Maria had been predicting when every baby would be due, what sex it would be, who would get what job, and who would marry whom—and not once had she truly nailed it. She would always explain the error away, of course, recrafting what the image in the grounds must have meant, and the rest of the family would respectfully buy it, but I just couldn't. I never thought to question her, as this was the way our family had always been, but by the time I was grown, I had caught on that something was not quite right, that maybe Theía Maria's "gift" wasn't what everyone believed it to be. Still, I would never have said a word about it, mostly out of respect for my mum.

Today's prediction was no surprise. Ever since I'd broken off the engagement my parents had loosely arranged for me when I was eighteen—because I chose college over marriage, because my fiancé's parents sat me down and gave me an ultimatum, because a good Greek girl could not be more educated than her husband—not surprisingly, I had become the mystic focus of Theía Maria's faulty readings. In fact, I'd become the biggest problem to solve that my aunts had ever encountered.

For the past few years, at every family gathering, which always included more aunts, uncles, and cousins than could ever fit in one house, the aunts huddled in the dining room or around the kitchen table discussing everyone's lives. Not their own, of course, but everyone else's, and mine in particular. There was nothing worse than going into the kitchen for another bite of baklava and overhearing my name and the ensuing conversation about my "plight" in life.

My "plight" was that, by good Greek girl standards, I was old. Very old. So old, it was unlikely anyone would ever want to marry me. This was beyond distressing to my mother. She had never understood me or known what to do with me. I had been unconventional from the start. When she wanted me to learn how to cook, I was huddled in a corner with a book. When she wanted me to learn ballet, I wanted to play soccer with the boys. When she wanted me to sit down and be quiet, I was more inclined to be a leader—at school, among all my friends, wherever I landed. Mum just wanted me to blend in, as good Greek girls were to be seen and not heard. But I had a voice, and like the aunts, I wasn't afraid to use it. Only I didn't use it or any of the attributes God had given me the way any of them had hoped. Therein lie all the challenges, and why my aunts took it upon themselves to salvage my life. Albeit with faulty coffee bean residue.

No sooner had Theía Maria finished her prediction of my future than all of them in unison aimed their wishful and superstitious seal of approval in my direction: "Ftou! Ftou! Ftou!" Though no real spittle landed on me, spitting was their way of sealing the deal, of warding off the evil none of them wanted to befall me. They were desperate to see me married, and somehow all this mumbo jumbo was their way of getting me to the altar and on to having babies. Lots of babies. Because that's what good Greek girls did.

I was never sure whether to laugh hysterically or cry at how hurtful it felt to think that every grown woman in my family thought my ovaries were over and done. Forever. But of course, out of respect, especially for my mother, I never did either. We were Greek. And this was how it had always been. Loud. Crazy. Superstitious. Religious. With loads of food. And spitting. Always spitting.

Several years later, when I finally did marry, like all the aunts, Theía Maria was relieved, and she couldn't resist taking all the credit. She was convinced she'd seen my love life play out in the bottom of a cup. I couldn't help but laugh because, for once, she might have accidently gotten one or two things right. Though Nick wasn't "one of our own," as he wasn't Greek but English; though he wasn't "close but from far away," as he was as Australian as I was; though he didn't step into my life "with a great fortune," as in the beginning we weren't always sure how we'd make it; he was, as she had said, exactly what I needed— and he didn't mind my age at all. I was just shy of thirty on our wedding day, way over the hill for a good Greek girl, and Nick loved me anyway.

IF ONLY WE HAD KNOWN TO PRAY

When I was growing up, all my family went to church regularly. In fact, going to church was as much a part of who we were as the Greek blood flowing in our veins. But from my experience, our Greek culture and traditions had more influence in our lives than church did. When it came to the issues of life, including getting me married off, everyone tackled the problem with a little bit of church and whole lot of superstition. Instead of praying to God first, for example, what I remember most is Theía Maria's antics or everyone spitting or Mum reaching for the saltshaker so she could throw some salt over her shoulder—or, of course, all my aunts talking for hours on end to one another, as though the more talking they did the more likely they were to resolve every problem they saw, mine in particular. I certainly can't remember us ever taking one another's hands and going to God for his help. In fact, I cannot recollect anyone in my family ever suggesting we stop and pray about anything.

Our house was full of icons—Jesus, Mary, and many of the saints—and I occasionally caught my mum lighting a candle or burning incense. Still, I never heard her pray. I was taught formal prayers that we memorized in ancient Greek and then spoke at all the correlating events in life—births, deaths, baptisms, communions, confirmations—but I may as well have been reciting the phone book each time because I was saying words in a language I never knew. How could I? At home we spoke modern and not ancient Greek. Though I could recite the prayers, I understood none of them.

At church, the only person I saw pray was the priest. The service lasted for three hours, and he chanted in ancient Greek the entire time. So I really had no idea what he was saying, but at some point I assumed he prayed because he did close his eyes and turn his face heavenward. In my childlike mind, I think from watching him, I deduced he had a hotline to God and the rest of us were left to work it out as best we could. I was left with the impression that God was a big God who was too busy running an entire universe to have time for regular people like me. I never felt holy or worthy or important enough to think I could directly commune with God. I certainly don't remember ever being encouraged to talk to God directly, and definitely not in my own words.

I imagine this all might sound strange, unless, of course, you grew up in a Greek culture as steeped in traditions and superstitions as I did. But looking back, I can understand why my family reached for superstitious practices more than they reached for God. None of us understood the personal and relational side of God. We had no idea he wanted to interact with us. It was clear to me that I should confess to God when I sinned—which was quite often for me, as I could be quite the little stinker—but to think God longed to have a relationship with me and that relationship could be cultivated through prayer never would have occurred to me. All the formal prayers we memorized and recited in a formal church setting led me to believe that prayer was a formal designated thing for a formal designated time. To me, faith was not a personal or intimate relationship that could be nurtured and further developed through communication with God, through being present with him, in any setting, at any time of the day or night. I just never thought of things that way.

Maybe you didn't either. Or maybe you did. But what about now? Do you think God wants to hear from you? That he wants you to cultivate a relationship with him through prayer? I'm not saying you have to spend as many hours a day talking to God as my aunts did to one another, but do you spend time praying to God before you start your day? Or as you go through your day? About all the things going on in your day? Or do you find yourself talking to others more? Wanting their opinions more? Wondering what their spiritual take is on it all?

Looking back and thinking of my aunts gathered around the

kitchen table, I can see how natural it is for us to want to talk to people we can see rather than to a God we can't see. Still, God wants us talking to him more than anyone else. It's one more link in our chain that keeps us anchored to him, so we don't find ourselves drifting away from him.

THE DAY CAROL PRAYED

I'll never forget the first time I got a glimpse of someone praying who wasn't a priest. I was just fourteen at the time, taking religion classes in school, and I watched and listened as a woman prayed—in English, no less. It was the 1980s, and religious education was a compulsory requirement in Australia's school system. When there weren't enough teachers, mums were recruited to teach us. The mum who taught me was Carol, and her depiction of what a life in Christ looked like was far different from what I had been raised to understand. I grew up knowing who Jesus was, of course; in fact, he was gloriously depicted with statues, on stained-glass windows, on prayer cards, and in books. But the Jesus I knew was more of an icon than anything else, one that was comfortably placed on the mantel right next to a replica of the Parthenon. In our house, the local healer was more likely to be called on than Jesus—someone known for helping break the curse of the evil eye, something no Greek ever wanted to befall them.

Carol had been saved in the seventies, in the age of the Jesus Movement and coffee-shop revivals, and week after week, I sat mesmerized, listening to her stories of how Jesus radically changed her life. She had been a biker, addicted to drugs, and was dropping acid when Jesus got her attention. At the time, I wasn't entirely sure what acid was, but I could tell from what she said that it was something to definitely steer away from. From what she described, I deduced that hallucinations weren't a good thing, even if you did think you saw Jesus in the midst of them.[1]

Every Tuesday, after she shuttled her three kids off to their schools, she showed up at ours and taught us what she knew. It wasn't volumes, and certainly not anything you would expect from someone with a seminary education, but it was enough to captivate me and a handful of my friends. As you can imagine, most of the twenty or so kids in my class were utterly bored. Some kids even slept through the class, but I couldn't keep my eyes off Carol. She had me hanging on her every word. Besides, not everyone had a real-life hippie who had experienced hallucinations for a religion teacher!

What caught my attention most was that Carol started and ended every class time with prayer. I had never heard anyone talk to the God of the universe as if he was their best friend. And when Carol prayed, she sounded so normal. She didn't have some weird voice saved especially for churchy things. Instead, she just talked to Jesus. Like she really knew him. Like she really meant the words she prayed. Like she wanted to talk to him more than anyone else.

For a young girl who probably got spat on as she was leaving the house for school that day, the idea of talking to Jesus, and then expecting him to communicate back in some way, was profound. I had grown up thinking he was too busy with all the big things in this world to ever have time for me, but Carol prayed as though she expected him to have time for her and for us all. Carol seemed to think Jesus cared personally and intimately about every one of us—and that he knew all about us. That was revolutionary to me. How could I not at least consider praying to a God like that?

PRAYER IS FULL ACCESS

Carol made prayer so understandable for me. So relatable. Listening to her pray, it seemed like a conversation. It made me want to talk to a God who seemed to want to listen to me. Scottish Reformer John Knox called prayer "an earnest and familiar talking with God."[2] I think he hit the nail on the head.

I understand, depending on our spiritual upbringing, that prayer can sound lofty or even boring, but it is in prayer that we learn how to trust him. It is in prayer that we remember God is great, sovereign, and all-powerful. It is in prayer that we can bring our concerns, anxieties, worries, and cares to God. That we can pour out our hearts to God. It is in prayer that we confess our sins and receive forgiveness. It is in prayer that we can ask for wisdom, help, knowledge, understanding, strength, and courage. It is in prayer that we can ask God to meet all our needs. It is in prayer that we can do spiritual warfare. That we can do battle and prevail in his power. It is in prayer that we can give thanks to, worship, and praise God. It is in prayer that we can be still and wait on God. That we can listen. That we can develop intimacy with God. That we can get to know him and feel known by him. Isn't that what we are all looking for? To be seen? To be heard? To be known? To be loved? Being in close proximity to someone regularly is a huge component in keeping us from drifting away from them. In keeping us anchored emotionally with them. So it is with us and God through prayer.

Prayer is a privilege. An honor. A delight. Talking to and listening to our heavenly Father, with nothing and no one standing between us, is something we *get* to do. Having grown up in a world where I failed to realize that I could talk straight to God, that nothing could separate me from the presence of God (Rom. 8:31–39), this was astounding to me. I had no idea that when Jesus died on the cross, the veil in the temple was "torn in two" (Matt. 27:51), much less what it meant. Later, I learned the veil was a curtain in the temple separating the people from the holy of holies, where the earthly presence of God dwelt.[3] Right after Jesus' death, the veil literally split from top to bottom, meaning that any and all go-betweens, like Old Testament priests, New Testament religious leaders, even the priests I had grown up learning from and listening to, were no longer necessary for me to talk to God.

Do you realize what this means for you and me today? As children of God, we can run to the very throne of God. The writer of Hebrews said, "Let us then approach God's throne of grace with confidence, so that we may receive mercy and find grace to help us in our time of need" (4:16 NIV).

That means we have access! Like a full backstage pass. The God of the universe, the One who flung the stars into the sky, the One who spoke it all into existence, the One who is all-knowing, all-powerful, and ever present, has given us access to be with him, any time of the day or night. Because he wants to be with us! Connected to us. We literally have an open invitation to run to the throne room,

> Prayer is a privilege. An honor. A delight. Talking to and listening to our heavenly Father, with nothing and no one standing between us, is something we *get* to do.

full of confidence that God wants to hear what we have to say. There is nothing—no mistake, no past, no sin, no person, no shame—that can block our access to God.

Can you feel the magnitude of what this means? Nothing can keep you away from God. Nothing. Just like when my girls were little and they'd run into our bedroom in the morning and jump into bed with Nick and me, so we can run to our heavenly Father. We never would have pushed our girls away. We never would have locked the door and left them in the hall begging to get in. Instead, we gave them free access. We were delighted they felt the freedom to come running.

I have to admit, though, as they've grown older, they don't come bouncing in as much. Not like they used to. They've grown into teenagers who sleep half the day anytime they get a chance. I love the stage they're in now. We have the most amazing conversations, and when Nick and I are traveling, we constantly FaceTime and text with them. It's how we all continue to stay connected to one another, so we don't drift apart as a family. Staying in communication keeps us close and on the same page. It keeps us up-to-date on everything going on in our lives. But to be honest, I miss them being little and running into our room, jumping on our bed.

RUN TO GOD

If the avenue of prayer keeps us anchored in an intimate relationship with God, then perhaps when we find our communication with God becoming less frequent, less prioritized, less transparent, less vital, we can safely assume we are drifting. When we find that we are moving away from dependence on God to self-reliance and independence apart from him, then we are drifting.

Martin Luther, the German priest and theologian who sparked the Protestant Reformation, once said, "To be a Christian without prayer is no more possible than to be alive without breathing." From my experience, I couldn't agree more. When it comes to drifting, prayer is one of the practices that keeps us the most anchored. I say this because we see in Scripture that Jesus stayed connected to his heavenly Father through prayer. He prayed when he was alone (Matt. 26:36–44). He prayed when he was with people (Luke 10:21). He prayed before eating (Matt. 15:36; 26:26; Luke 24:30; John 6:11), traveling, and making important decisions—like when he prayed all night before choosing his twelve disciples (Luke 6:12–13). He prayed before, during, and after healing people (Mark 7:34–35; Luke 5:12–16; John 11: 41–42). He prayed for himself (John 17:1–5), for his disciples (Luke 22:31–32; John 17:6–19), and for all believers (Matt. 19:13–15; John 17:20–26). He prayed for his Father's will (Luke 22:42). He prayed for others to be forgiven (Luke 23:34). He prayed in his pain and in his suffering (Matt. 27:46). And what's especially astounding to me, to this day, he hasn't stopped praying; he ever lives to make intercession for you and for me (Heb. 7:25).

> When it comes to drifting, prayer is one of the practices that keeps us the most anchored.

But for us—though we all want to be like Jesus—letting go of prayer can happen so easily. We can get busy, forgetful, or distracted, and before we know it, we can start viewing prayer as a last resort or an activity to fit in—if and where it does—versus a time to connect with the One we love . . . and who loves us. Or if we feel disappointed or discouraged with God, or even angry with him, then it's easy to let a day go by without praying, and for that day to become a week, and that week to become a month, and before we realize it, the months have grown into a year.

Have you ever wondered how much God misses us when we drift away from him? When we stop running to his throne of grace like we used to? Jumping into his arms. Telling him all about our day and our dreams, our cares and our concerns, our joy and our victories. Telling him all about the people we love and the people whom we desperately want to know him the way we know him. Pouring out our hearts to him when we feel blindsided by heart-wrenching moments we never saw coming. Trusting him when we don't understand what's happening or why. Leaning into his comfort on our darkest days.

I wonder how he feels when we pull back, though the answer is in the pages of Scripture. So many times, over thousands of years, he has said to his people, "Return to me" (Neh. 1:9; Hosea 6:1, 14:1; Zech. 1:3) or "Come back to me" or, to those who don't know him, "Come to me" (Matt. 11:28; John 6:37). The whole of Scripture reveals God's heart—from creation to our being a new creation—of his desire for relationship, of his unending love for us.

All of us know the pain of having someone we love pull away. And the truth is, God has experienced this more frequently—and at a greater level—than any of us ever have. Still, he loves us. He reaches for us. He pursues us, no matter why we've drifted.

Sometimes, when we feel he hasn't come through for us or answered our prayers the way we had hoped, it's easy to want to quit talking to God, just like we naturally want to withdraw and quit talking to people who disappoint us, who don't come through for us. It's as though the same reasons we run to God in prayer can be the same reasons we drift away.

I know what it's like not to have prayer answered the way I hoped. I'm sure you know what that's like too. Even the members of the early church knew what that was like. At a time when the church was absolutely flourishing, King Herod Agrippa wanted the favor of the Jewish people and their leaders—at any cost.[4] So he went after the Christians to persecute them, including two of the apostles who had been especially close to Jesus. He had James arrested first—and then beheaded (Acts 12:2). Next, he had Peter arrested (v. 3)—and this was for the third time. The first two times, Peter had been set free (Acts 4:7–21; 5:18–20), so on this third occasion, Herod put him under maximum security, with sixteen soldiers taking shifts to guard him. Two at a time were even shackled to Peter (12:4–6). Herod knew these Christians had a way of escaping. They either rose from the dead like Jesus or were rescued like Peter by angels. Either way, he wasn't taking any chances this time.

But then, the night before Peter was to stand trial, an angel appeared and walked Peter out of that prison (vv. 7–10). Once again, he was miraculously set free.

What I want us to focus on here is how, the whole time this miracle was happening, the church was praying (v. 12). Earnestly. Fervently. Even though not everything was as they hoped. James was now dead. And Peter was alive but imprisoned yet again. The early church was heartbroken, but when they could have grown discouraged, despondent, angry, or hard-hearted, they kept praying. They didn't seem to have a faith dilemma with James dying and Peter living. They seemed to understand that prayer is predicated on trust in God, even when we don't understand what he is doing.

More than two thousand years later, I don't know why some people live and some don't. I don't know why things we pray so hard about don't always work out. I don't know why unimaginable heartache and tragedy happen, despite our best efforts in prayer. Despite getting everyone we know to pray with us and for us. I would imagine that we all have a James in our lives. The person who died instead of being healed. The child who went further away instead of being drawn closer to God. The marriage that fell apart instead of being glued back together. The investment that went belly-up instead of padding our retirement. The job that let us go instead of promoting us as we'd hoped.

What is your James? Is there a reason why you quit believing that prayer can change things? Is there a reason why you might not be running to God with the same kind of faith the way you once did? With the same fervor you once had?

Whatever the reason, when we find ourselves not wanting to talk to Jesus as much as we once did, or for as long as we once did; when we find ourselves wanting to talk more to people than Jesus, we're drifting. If we're thinking more than we're praying, posting more than we're praying, venting more than we're praying, even asking others to pray for us more than we're taking things to Jesus ourselves, then we're drifting—and it's time to run to Jesus once more.

PRAYER ANCHORS US

One of my favorite places to pray is walking along the beach—any beach anywhere in the world. Whether I'm at home in California walking alongside the Pacific or near our offices in

Greece soaking in the Mediterranean Sea or in Cape Town, South Africa, hiking in full view of the Atlantic, I walk, and I pray. I talk aloud to God, confessing my sins, petitioning him with my requests, and telling him of others I know needing help, answers, and guidance. I remind him of what he's called me to do and how he's promised to help me fulfill my purpose. I thank him as he reorients my perspective and helps me see things the way he does. I tell him how grateful I am. For Nick. For our girls. For our team. For the work he's put before us. I focus heavenward, worshipping him, offering to him all my adoration. Offering him all of me.

Each time I pray these ways, I don't do it in any particular order. I don't feel given to a formula of prayer, but more to a relationship in prayer. A conversation between me and God.

I pray when I'm happy. I pray when I'm sad. I pray when I'm rested. I pray when I'm tired. I pray when I'm at home. I pray when I'm on a plane. I pray when I need answers, and I pray when I just need reassurance. I pray when it's easy, and I pray when it's hard. I even pray when it feels like God isn't listening to me. When no matter how hard I try to hear him, all I feel is silence. Rather than take his silence as rejection, disapproval, or indifference and give him the silent treatment, I pray. Rather than judge him as not caring, I pray. No matter what's going on, no matter where in the world I am, no matter what time of day it is, when something comes up in my heart or crosses my mind, I pray.

Prayer is a declaration of dependence. It's our way of saying, "God, I want you. I need you." When we bring something to God in prayer, we are saying, "God, I want your rule, I want your reign, I want your direction, I want your will, I want your help in this. I want you in this." And every time we withhold from God, we are also making a statement: "God, I'm good. I've got this" or

"God, to be honest, I'm not all that interested in what you have to say about this." When you are tempted to pass by the secret place of prayer, when you are tempted to leave something off the table, out of your conversation with him, ask yourself, *Do I want to go at this without him?* There is no good, no life in that, since he is life. To turn to God in prayer is to involve him, to include him, to cling to him.

If I didn't pray, I would drift. Even when I found myself wanting to ring the bell, when I felt as though I was going through one of the hardest times of my ministry life, when I didn't feel like I had the strength to pray, I prayed. So many times in that season, I didn't feel like my prayers mattered. It felt as if they were bouncing off the ceiling. Like I was talking to myself and no one else. Like praying was a waste of time. That it wasn't doing a bit of good. Still, I prayed. Admittedly, during that season it was more like I groaned, I cried, I lamented, I yelled, I even had a tantrum or two, but I kept going to God. I figure it still falls under the category of prayer. I remember saying to Nick one day, "Well, at least I'm still tethered to God because I'm still talking to him, albeit with a little yelling."

Before you judge me, don't forget that even King David—you know, the guy after God's own heart—once prayed, "How long, LORD? Will you forget me forever? How long will you hide your face from me? How long will I store up anxious concerns within me, agony in my mind every day? How long will my enemy dominate me?" (Ps. 13:1–2).

Isn't it good to know that no matter how big a tantrum we throw, God doesn't walk away? To this day, when I pray, I am so honest with God. With him, I am my truest self. I understand that self may be too much for people, but it is never too

> When I pray, I am so honest with God. With him, I am my truest self. I understand that self may be too much for people, but it is never too much for God.

much for God. He knows everything that is happening in me and to me. He knows what's weighing on my heart and mind. There's no hiding any of it from him. Still, he just wants me to be honest and say it. He wants us all to say it. God can handle whatever we pour out, however we do it. He doesn't want us to bottle things up. Whatever we're feeling, he doesn't want us to stuff it, suppress it, or internalize it. That will only cause us to drift. Instead, God wants us to pour out our hearts to him. He wants us to pray.

What are we supposed to pray about? All things (Phil. 4:6).

When are we supposed to pray? All the time (1 Thess. 5:16–18).

All things . . . all the time. Is there something in the "all things" category of life that you need to bring to him today? For the first time . . . or for the thousandth time?

Do you want more of him today? Pray today!

Is wisdom or direction needed today? Pray today!

Are enemies encompassing today? Pray today!

Is forgiveness needed today? Pray today!

Is temptation pressing today? Pray today!

Does a relationship need reconciliation today? Pray today!

Do you need a breakthrough in some area today? Pray today!

Are resources short today? Pray today!

Is healing, peace, or salvation needed today? Pray today!

Does a stronghold need to be broken today? Pray today!

Have you been told it's impossible today? Pray today!

As my friend Rebekah Layton says, prayer is both a grace and a gain: a grace that keeps us anchored to him and a gain that advances his rule and reign.

Our God loves to be sought. Our God is a good Father. Our God does the impossible. Our God is so, so faithful . . . faithful to hear, faithful to answer. May we be faithful. Faithful to believe him. To believe he hears. And faithful to pursue him in the place of prayer. Because we need him. Because we love him. Because we want him. Because we long for him and his kingdom to come. Because we do not want to drift.

6

YOU STOP GATHERING AND YOU START ISOLATING

There is a difference between solitude and isolation.
One is connected and one isn't. Solitude replenishes,
isolation diminishes.

—HENRY CLOUD

Driving through the streets of Doha, Qatar, taking in all the sky-scrapers and majestic architecture, I thought the city looked as though it had risen straight up out of the sands of the Rub' al-Khali desert. Buildings sculpted like waves seemed to mimic the blue-green tide of the Persian Gulf coming ashore. Pristine boulevards lined with majestic palms outlined the entire cityscape, show-casing each design as though it were a work of art. As we moved closer to the heart of the city, the architecture continued to be one more modern wonder after the other, only now interspersed with a few more traditional Islamic designs, shorter stucco-looking structures awash in the soft desert hues of cream, yellow, and tan.

Nick and I had been here for a few days so I could speak at a leadership conference, and each time we rode through the city, the sights didn't disappoint. Today, we were on our way to a church where I had been invited to speak. We were being driven by Joseph, an expatriate living and working in the capital city, and his friend and colleague Samuel. The two of them were part of the minority population of Christians who made their home in this Middle Eastern country.

Joseph had been talking much of the time, telling us about the development of the city and the interesting facts visitors might want to know. The very kind of information I always love to learn everywhere I travel. And though I started out paying close attention to his every word, at some point, I couldn't help but grow distracted. My heart was full and overflowing, almost racing. With hope. With joy. With the thrill of watching God unfold what he was doing in his church in this part of the world. I hadn't even been able to sleep, and unlike most times when I travel internationally, it wasn't because of jet lag. Deep down, I didn't want to miss anything that might be happening, much like a kid the night before a summer vacation.

Still staring out the window at the passing blur of buildings and people, at cars and city life, I thought about how much this part of the world was woven into the story of my ancestors. Both of my parents had been born into Greek families in Alexandria, Egypt, though they didn't meet each other until after they immigrated to Australia. It was the generation before them, the ones who had fled Greece and Turkey after the Greek genocide of 1922, that caused much of my family to be there. Because my parents grew up in Egypt, they both spoke Arabic fluently, a gift they especially enjoyed when they didn't want my brothers and me to know what they were saying. I can still remember trying my best to decode all the syllables I heard, determined to figure out what they might be keeping from us, though I never succeeded. Despite moving to Australia, my parents never let go of their Greek heritage, or the obvious influence of being born and raised in the Middle East. Even our dinner table and Sunday get-togethers reflected the mix of foods that they loved. Falafel. Dolma. Kushari. Baklava. It was always the best of both worlds. I've often thought that my heritage probably explains why, for as long as I can remember, I've had such a tender place in my heart for the Middle East.

As we were drawing closer to the outskirts of the city, it caught my ear that Joseph was beginning to share more of his personal story and less about the city. His extended family had lived in Qatar for roughly thirty years, he said, as expatriates from India working in the petrochemical industry so prevalent throughout the Middle East. They were Christians, but for the first fifteen years they lived in the country, they had not been allowed to express their faith in any way. No Christian had. Not publicly. Not at work. Nor at home. At one point, Samuel briefly interjected, recounting how his family had known people who did so, and how they had lost their jobs, were made to leave the country, or were put in jail.

Joseph went on to explain that only in the last fifteen years had they been allowed to gather in church meetings with other Christians. Certain approved Christian denominations had been granted permission to build church buildings, but only within a highly fortified and designated religious complex set beyond the outskirts of the city.[1] There were strict rules associated with when Christians could gather and for how long, and every one of them had to be registered to have permission to enter the religious complex. Still, Joseph said that because being able to attend a church gathering made him feel far more connected to the body of Christ, it made the drive and jumping through all of the hoops to get there completely worth it.

No sooner had Joseph mentioned the complex than I caught a glimpse of it in the distance. It appeared to be a walled compound stretching out into the desert, with buildings peeking out over the perimeter. As we drew closer to the entrance, I saw tall, chain-link gates manned with officials, much like a checkpoint at a military base. Apparently, we would have to stop before being allowed to enter.

Reaching the gate, Joseph showed a form of identification, as well as a special permit for me, since I was the guest speaker in one of the churches that day. Only when the official asked each of us if we were Christians and we showed our passports were we granted entry to the complex. Joseph explained that any other time he would have had to park much farther away from the compound and walk in the blistering desert heat to reach the checkpoint. In fact, he said this was the first time he had ever driven through the gate. I couldn't help but notice all the people coming and going. They all looked so happy. So glad to be here.

Moving forward through the compound, Joseph pointed out the different churches. Catholic. Greek Orthodox. Coptic. Baptist. Assemblies of God. On and on they went. I later learned that the Catholic church was not only the first built among these but also the first church ever built in the past fourteen centuries in Doha.[2]

As we passed by even more buildings inside other walled-in areas, Joseph pointed out ones reflecting large traditional Christian faiths from Africa, the Philippines, and India. When I asked why all the buildings looked so similar, because I wasn't really able to tell one from another just by looking at them, Joseph explained how the designs were government restricted. None of them were allowed to display any of the telltale signs of Christian houses of worship. No crosses. No steeples. No bells. Though he said a few had faint airbrushed images on the inside.[3]

Once inside, Nick and I worshipped with the small crowd that had gathered in the room where we were—and with all the other people who were spread throughout all the buildings in the complex. When I took a moment and scanned the crowd, people's faces seemed to say it all. They wanted to be here worshipping God more than anywhere else on the planet. And nothing, not the chain-link gates, the desert heat, or the strict restrictions, could keep them from it. I couldn't help but feel the exact same way.

THE FREEDOM TO GATHER

Church is church, the world over. I have had the privilege of ministering in local churches in more than fifty nations. Some have gathered in huge auditoriums seating thousands of people, others in far smaller sanctuaries—places that have included everything from movie theaters to community centers to warehouses to schools to homes. I've even been with members of the underground church in China. At the heart of every gathering has always been the power of people united in worship, lifting up King Jesus together. People leaning in to hear his Word preached, pray for one another, fellowship with one another, break bread together, study the Scriptures together, and rejoice at seeing one another baptized. There is something so unique and powerful that happens when the body of Christ gathers together. Our day in Qatar was no exception.

Still, I couldn't let go of the reality that it isn't easy being a follower of Jesus in this part of the world, where just over 10 percent of the population is Christian.[4] I grew up in Australia, and now live in the USA, so I have always known freedom of religion. I have never lived in a nation that didn't allow me to gather with Christians anywhere I wanted whenever I wanted. I have never lived somewhere that didn't allow religious symbols to be displayed publicly—even on my desk at work—or to be depicted on buildings, signifying to everyone that it was a house of worship.

Once the service was over, Nick and I went to lunch with several couples from the church because, well, hummus, manakeesh, and tabbouleh were waiting. Our conversation turned to the challenges that these dear brothers and sisters in Christ faced as Christians in this region of the world, and especially the ones faced by those who chose to actually go to church and gather openly with other believers. I couldn't help but wonder why they still wanted to go, particularly when it would have been so much easier and safer to stay home. Only a year before there had been a terrorist attack on the religious complex. I could only imagine what must have gone through their minds every time they walked through the security checkpoint. I really wondered if I would still go to church with my family under such conditions. I'd like to think I was that courageous, but during our lunch, I discovered that these Middle

Eastern Christians had a strength and passion I envied. They were full of love, joy, and peace, openly sharing stories with us about people in their church community. They were just so grateful that they could meet together, no matter how great the cost.

Listening to their stories made me think of the Jewish Christians in the early church, the ones mentioned in the book of Hebrews. It gave me a little more insight into what it might have felt like for them when the author of Hebrews wrote to them, urging them to continue meeting, despite the obstacles they would have to overcome.

They were living in a culture where the majority of people weren't followers of Jesus, just like it was in Doha, and because they wanted to express their faith, they were being threatened and persecuted. They were losing their property, being shunned in their communities, and some were even martyred (10:33–34). Fearful of meeting, they retreated from gathering, many of them hiding out in their homes, others scattering to the surrounding countryside, all because getting together could cost them their lives.[5] But in spite of the danger, in spite of their fear, the writer of Hebrews urged them, "Let us consider one another in order to provoke love and good works, not neglecting to gather together, as some are in the habit of doing, but encouraging each other, and all the more as you see the day approaching" (10:24–25).

It is astounding to me that despite all of the obvious risks involved in gathering as believers to worship Jesus during those days, the benefits must have outweighed the risks. The writer to the Hebrews could have said, "Stay home, don't gather, do all you can to protect yourselves." But instead he said the opposite: "Do not neglect to gather."

For the writer to the Hebrews to say, "Do not neglect to

gather," implies that there is a benefit we get from gathering that we would not get if we did not take the time to do so. Since we have already established that all you have to do to drift is nothing, then perhaps neglecting to gather is one more way that we can be prone to drifting. In other words, when it comes to church, we don't have to do anything ungodly to find ourselves drifting; all we have to do is simply neglect to gather. But as Matt Merker wrote during the pandemic of 2020 in an article titled "Why Gather? Thinking About Gathering When Churches Can't," gathering isn't just what the church does; it's part of what the church *is*. God saved us as individuals to collectively be a corporate assembly.[6] In the original Greek, the word for "assembly" is *ekklesia*.[7] According to Merker, it's "the same word the New Testament writers used to refer to the local church. It's simply the term for a gathering. But when applied to the church, it carries the rich Old Testament connotation of standing together as God's chosen people."[8]

I've heard it said that the church is a people, not a place. I feel sure I've even said something along those lines before. It's true that a church remains a church even when it's not gathered, but think of it like this: My daughter Catherine played volleyball in high school. She tried out and was awarded a position on the team. From that point on, she was on the team twenty-four seven. Even when she and her fellow team members weren't gathered, they were collectively considered the team. Still, none of the girls could be on the team and never show up for the games. They had to participate. They had to come together to

> We don't have to do anything ungodly to find ourselves drifting; all we have to do is simply neglect to gather.

practice and then compete in games. In the same way, the church is a people, but it's also a place because a church becomes a church when members gather and participate in that place.[9] I understand that church, of course, is more than a gathering, but as Merker also said, it is never less.[10]

When the church gathers in corporate worship, those in the congregation make themselves visible to one another. Theologian Everett Ferguson said it this way: "In assembly, the church becomes itself. It becomes conscious of itself, confesses itself to be a distinctive entity, shows itself to be what it is—a community (a people) gathered by the grace of God, dependent on him, and honoring him. The assembly allows the church to emerge in its true nature."[11]

As the church, we were created to gather, then scatter, then gather again.[12] There is purpose in our gathering and in our scattering. We need both. Not just one or the other.

This is part of what I never grasped as a kid. I had to go to church every Sunday because my parents forced me. To be Greek was to be Orthodox, and going to church was a cultural expectation, especially since we were part of an immigrant community in a foreign land. Getting together at our local Greek Orthodox church was the central weekly meeting place for most of the Greek immigrants in our city. Not going to church simply would never have been an option. Because the priest spoke in ancient Greek, I never understood what was going on, so it never occurred to me that what happened in church on Sunday could have any impact on my Monday, Tuesday, Wednesday, Thursday, Friday, or Saturday. Church had no real relevance in my life. It was something that meant everything to my parents, but from my vantage point, it seemed as if it was more for cultural reasons than for spiritual ones. It's no wonder that as soon as I reached my midteens and was allowed to make more choices for myself, I stopped going.

I had no idea what the writer of Hebrews meant when he wrote, "Do not neglect to gather." I had no idea that going to church wasn't because of a religious or cultural obligation. I had no idea how important it was. I didn't fully understand that church is where we get to worship and express our adoration of God (Ps. 150:6; John 4:23–24). That church is where we get to learn how to put God and his kingdom first and to imitate Christ (Matt. 6:33; 1 Cor. 11:1; Eph. 5:1–2). That it is in church we gain an understanding of Scripture and how to live it, as well as discover God's guidance for our lives (Prov. 11:14; 24:6; Col. 3:16; 2 Tim. 3:16). It is in church that we fellowship with Jesus and with our heavenly Father and we find friendship with other Christians (Acts 2:42–47; Gal. 6:2; 1 John 1:3). It is in church that we exercise our gifts, serve one another, and have the joy of seeing God change lives and eternities as we serve (Rom. 12:4–8; 1 Cor. 12:26–27).[13]

What's more, beyond how church affects us personally, the church is the visible representation of God on the earth. When we gather, Jesus sanctifies the space; he shows up! "For where two or three are gathered together in my name, I am there among them" (Matt. 18:20). As Jonathan Leeman wrote in his essay, "The Church Gathered," all throughout Scripture the people came together in an assembly, in a tent, in a temple, as a church.[14] By coming together physically, they made God's kingdom visible in this earthly realm. Isn't that what we do to this day?

Leeman also wrote that when we gather as the church, we gather as an outpost of heaven that is visible, audible, and touchable. After all, "Humans are physical creatures. Bodies matter. Space matters. Physical togetherness matters." So gathering as the church on a patch of geography matters just as much as being the church.[15]

When I met the leaders of the underground church in China, they took enormous risks to gather in secret but still did it. The church in Doha had to go to great lengths to gather outside the city, but they felt it was worth it. In both places, the Christians understood that there is something powerful in the gathering, that there are many purposes in the gathering. They understood that the church is not a building, but the scattered church is obviously strengthened when we gather inside one. In a multitude of ways. It's how we stay tethered, anchored to Jesus, and not drifting. Individually and collectively.

A CHURCH ON EVERY CORNER

A little more than twenty-four hours after we left Qatar, Nick and I were on our way to church once more, only this time, we were in Texas. The wonder of modern travel is that I can get on a plane in the Middle East and be in the United States sixteen hours later. I was to speak at a church in Houston—another city known for its oil and gas industry. Another city with towering skyscrapers and majestic palms. Another city that stretches all the way to the coast. Still, as we drove in and out of the shadows falling across the streets, shadows shaped by the rising sun and the downtown skyline, I couldn't help but notice how it stood in such stark contrast to the streets of Doha.

In city block after city block that stretched into mile after mile, it was as though every iconic Christian symbol couldn't get past me. Steeples. Bells. Stained-glass windows. Crosses of every shape and size. As Nick navigated our way, I couldn't miss the statues, the prayer gardens, the monuments, the giant digital blinking signs.

The irony of it all was not lost on me. No one was having to drive to the outskirts of town or to a nearby city to a compound for church. Instead, it felt like there was a church on almost every corner. I was in a city with almost two thousand churches, including more than thirty-five megachurches, so surely if anyone wanted to attend any one of them, they wouldn't have to drive far at all.[16] Can you imagine how many churches each person might pass on their way to their favorite church? Surely, it would have to be at least one. I know on our way I lost count.

Once we arrived, Nick and I walked in just as the worship team was kicking off the service. We couldn't help but look at one another and smile big. The team was starting with one of the songs we had sung with the church in Doha.

Half a world away, and the people of God were united in faith, united in worship, lifting their hearts up to God with the exact same song. When Jesus walked the earth, he said, "I will build my church" (Matt. 16:18). From one side of the world to the other, I had just witnessed that he was still doing exactly what he said he would do. And it was breathtaking.

THE COMMUNITY OF THE CHURCH

Everything I grew up thinking about church changed for me when I was twenty-two. A friend I met while volunteering at a local community youth center for at-risk kids invited me to his church. I remember him being so passionate that I had to go and find out how anyone could be so excited about something I had found utterly boring. When I walked in, I discovered something I had never known—people who were gathering because they wanted to. Because they couldn't wait to worship and learn and grow and share the love of Christ. Because they were willing to be scattered afterward and go find people like me—someone who needed to know that Jesus loved them, died for them, and rose again from the dead so that they could have forgiveness for their past, a fresh start here on earth, and an eternal hope for the future. I discovered people who truly understood the value of gathering—the gathering helped to strengthen and equip them for their scattering.

From that day forward, my understanding began to grow. Over time, church became family for me, and like every family, it has not been perfect, but it has been a haven and home. In church I started to deal with the pain of my broken past, and over time, I found healing and wholeness. I began building lifelong friendships, met and married my husband, Nick, and dedicated and raised our daughters in the same local church. There I fell in love with the Word of God and learned how to truly worship. I discovered my gifting and calling. I was discipled, loved, corrected, challenged, and released into ministry. In church I learned to love the lost, reach the lost, become active in the fight for justice and peace, advocate for the poor and the marginalized, and strengthen and empower women. I learned to appreciate and care for the planet God has given us. Through the years, I have struggled, laughed, cried, grieved, prayed, hoped, dreamed, despaired, suffered, rejoiced, and praised, all with my church family at my side—and at other times, I've had the privilege of being there to run alongside my church family when they were experiencing the same things.

The connection to my church family helped me stay anchored to Jesus—and not drift far from his purpose for my life. At the same time, I am not naive enough to think that my church experience is everyone's experience. I am well aware that for some people, the very word *church* causes them to recoil and pull back. You may even be one of these people and want to put this book down now because of your negative church experience. I get it, but please keep reading. You were on my heart as I was writing.

There is no doubt that for some, the church has been a poor witness of the love and grace of Jesus, for one reason or another. Maybe a leader they looked up to let them down. Maybe a position they held dear was given to someone else. Maybe someone in the children's ministry excluded their child. Maybe when their marriage dissolved, the people they thought would walk alongside them walked alongside their ex instead. Maybe it was something far worse.

I've had plenty of conversations with people who have been deeply wounded by other people in the church. Some have even asked me why I would spend my life building the very thing that has caused them such great pain. It's a valid question. Some have pointed out the flaws of the church throughout the ages as proof of its inherent faults.

It is true that many injustices have been done in the name of Christianity. History can't hide what has come to light throughout the centuries—the Dark Ages, the Crusades, the times the church didn't live up to its own standards. When it was plagued with corruption. When atrocities like war and famine and genocide occurred, and it looked the other way. Even in recent generations, the church has continued to grapple with so many issues, though none of them new—racism, sexism, abuse, materialism, greed, idolatry, nationalism, misogyny, legalism, judgmentalism. It is little wonder that some of you might feel done with the whole thing, not even wanting to darken the doors of a church. I get it. I really do.

I can't possibly know what each one of you may have gone through personally, or exactly how you feel, but I do know that though we are often hurt in community, we also heal in community. This includes the community of church. With all its flaws, quirks, challenges, and issues, the church is God's idea. And because the church is made up of people—and all of us on this side of eternity are flawed, imperfect people—there is no church that's not flawed.

> Though we are often hurt in community, we also heal in community. This includes the community of church.

YOU HAVE SOMETHING TO GIVE

Sometimes, the reason we stop gathering is far simpler. Perhaps you went on vacation, missed a few Sundays, and gradually just got out of the habit of going. Maybe you started a new job, and your schedule included working on Sundays. Maybe you moved and struggled to find a new church home. Maybe you started having to travel farther and more often for your kids' sports leagues. Maybe you feel like you don't get out of it what you once did. Or you prefer to watch online—something that's great when we can't get there in person. I'll never forget when watching online became our only option, when the pandemic hit and we had to shelter in place. I feel sure you remember it too. We were forced to isolate for our safety and protection—and for everyone else's. Perhaps, after that, you just never went back.

I feel sure there are more reasons than I could ever list, but it seems that some are more common than others. I cannot recollect how many times I have been asked, "Can I be a Christian and not go to church?" I always answer honestly: yes, of course. Nowhere in the Bible does it say you have to attend church to be a Christian. But of course, being a very passionate Greek woman, I want to hear the reason behind their question and then tell them about my own experience—with lots of humor, hand motions, and serious volume! I just can't help myself!

What I hope they eventually discover for themselves is that when we stop gathering, we start isolating, and when we start isolating, we become more susceptible to drifting—something that naturally leads to distance and distance to disconnection.[17]

Aren't you glad the writer of Hebrews gave us the antidote? "Do not neglect to gather." When we gather, it helps us to stay connected. To stay anchored. What's more, when we fail to gather, we miss not only all the blessings that come from gathering but also being a blessing to everyone else who has come to gather. We are one body with many parts, and we all have gifts to give. Have you ever wondered who might miss something because you were not there to give it? I know every time my daughters are not at the dinner table, I miss them! I miss what they add to the conversation—their witty observations, serious introspections, and fresh perspectives. I miss their off-the-wall humor. (I have no idea where they got that from!) For sure, I much prefer dinner with them than without them.

So it is with church. Church is about far more than just what we get out of it. It's about being in the body of Christ doing body life—together. When one of us is missing, it affects us all. What one of us does—or doesn't do—makes a difference. Paul wrote of this very idea in his letter to the church in Rome: "We have different gifts, according to the grace given to each of us. If your gift is prophesying, then prophesy in accordance with your faith; if it is serving, then serve; if it is teaching, then teach; if it is to encourage, then give encouragement; if it is giving, then give generously; if it is to lead, do it diligently; if it is to show mercy, do it cheerfully" (Rom. 12:6–8 NIV).

God wants us fulfilling our individual roles in the body. Participating. Contributing. Sometimes, I think we forget that going to church isn't just for us, but it's also for all the other people we will see there. It's not just about what we can get out of it, but what we can give while we're there.

When Catherine was just a baby, it was the grandmothers in the nursery who calmed my anxious first-time mother's heart. When I wasn't sure I wanted to leave her with complete strangers, when she would be crying and I would be about to, they were the ones who would assure me that she would be just fine, to go on to service and know that she would quit soon. The first few times, I wasn't sure whether to believe them. After all, they didn't know her like I did, but in the end, they were always right. Each time, when I would come back, there she'd be, sound asleep in someone's arms. Content. Peaceful. Happy as could be. It almost hurt my feelings that she didn't even miss me. To me, those women weren't just nursery workers; they were miracle workers. As Catherine grew from a baby to a toddler, from a toddler to a little girl, I asked those same women so many questions. When

Sophia came along, I kept asking questions. And they taught me so much, albeit mostly how to relax and enjoy church.

But what if they hadn't come? What if the nursery was full of uptight, first-time moms like me? I am so grateful they didn't think of themselves as women who already knew enough and didn't need to come to church. I'm so glad they still saw the value in giving of their gifts and fulfilling their purpose. I'm so glad they somehow instinctively knew to be contributors and not just consumers.

I could go on about how people in the church have continued to help me navigate all the ages and stages of my daughters' lives, because they have, but what's also important is what those women and so many others modeled before me about going to church and being the church. When they could have quit, they kept going, for my sake. They unselfishly came and gave of themselves to others.

ONE WHO IS ALWAYS WAITING

All of us have been in the position where we have been looking forward to a family member or friend coming to visit. I can think of many times when I have looked forward to a loved one coming and how I celebrated Greek-style when they arrived—meaning loud and with lots of food. I can also think of times when things didn't work out as planned, and I was left missing the one who I had prepared for and hoped would visit.

When it comes to us gathering together, I am convinced that no one looks forward to it more than God himself. While it is true that, through faith in Jesus Christ, every believer is indwelt by God's Spirit and has direct access to God, something else is also true: "In him [Jesus Christ] you also are being built together into a dwelling place for God by the Spirit" (Eph. 2:22 ESV). The "you" in this verse is plural, not singular. You *together* are a dwelling place for God. Remember, Jesus said, "For where two or three gather in my name, there am I with them" (Matt. 18:20 NIV). The truth is this: There is a special grace when we gather. There is a special way that God takes residence in our midst when we gather. Our gathering together does not just happen in God's name, but also in God's presence. And God is not the guest at his gatherings—we are.

The letters to the churches in the book of Revelation reveal that God is not only aware of but also cares deeply about each and every gathering around the globe. The ones in Qatar. The ones in Texas. The ones in cities. The ones in villages. The ones that are well known. The ones that aren't. The ones that meet freely. The ones that are forced underground. The one where you might be going every week. Each one is filled with people Jesus gave his life to save. And each one is a place God chooses to make his home. Each one helps us to stay tethered to Jesus. Each one helps us to keep from drifting.

> There is a special grace when we gather. There is a special way that God takes residence in our midst when we gather.

Are you connected to a local gathering? If you are, then keep going and plant your roots even deeper! If you aren't, then I want to encourage you to consider going to one. I know it might not be easy for you, but it could be the missing link in your chain that will help connect you more deeply to your anchor, Jesus. God is looking, longing, and waiting for your arrival, and so are others—others you need and others who need you.

7

YOU STOP HUNGERING AND
YOU START GORGING

If I find in myself a desire which no experience in this world can satisfy, the most probable explanation is that I was made for another world.

—C. S. LEWIS, *MERE CHRISTIANITY*

"Mum, I'm going to die. I just know it. I have to eat some Goldfish or graham crackers or ice cream or something. I can't go on like this. My body wasn't made to endure this. Why didn't we keep some emergency snacks? Catherine is suffering too. You're our mum. You are supposed to love us. God doesn't want us to suffer. Not like this. I'm convinced of it."

All I could do was laugh. It hadn't been even three full days since Team Caine had kicked all the bad carbs out of our house, and Sophia was caving. I had just come in the door and was walking through the living room when I spied her half lying on the couch and half falling off it. Ever the actor, she had the back of her hand resting across her forehead, as though she had fainted from the withdrawals, and was really embracing her character and the scene. Her sense of humor is always off the charts and one of the many things I love about her. She could make any moment a funny one. Even when she was feigning her last act.

"I feel sure you will live," I said. "Besides, there are far worse things to die from."

"There are?" she asked bleakly. "I can't imagine any right now."

This was going to be a long week. I could feel it already. Maybe a long month. Maybe a long few months.

Walking on through to the kitchen, I glanced over into the den, and there was Catherine. Sprawled out on the rug. Just staring up at the ceiling.

"Catherine, are you all right?" I ventured, bracing myself for the inevitable.

"It depends on how you define *all right*. I'm alive. But barely. I googled it, and I have every symptom you're supposed to have at this point. Sugar cravings. A headache. Brain fog. You do want me to excel in school, right? How am I supposed to do that with brain fog? One article I read said you're to treat brain fog with hormones."

"That's a whole different kind of brain fog, Catherine," I said, doing my best not to lose it completely. "The kind that women get when they're older. You know, older like me."

"Oh . . ." She caught on. "Well, I'm with Sophia. We need Goldfish. I could drive us to get some, but I know we all committed to this. What were we thinking? Are we sure we thought this all through well enough? Maybe we just got caught up in a euphoric family high and had a serious lapse of judgment."

By now, I couldn't stop laughing. I had dealt with my own symptoms all day—mostly just the inability to stop thinking about (obsessing about) how I couldn't have a piece of bread, the staple food of any Greek—but I wasn't about to admit this to either of my waning children.

"This is good for us!" I shouted. "We're going to be healthier. We're doing it together. We're cheering Dad on and helping him win his race. We're Team Caine! We're in it to win it! We're champions! We are more than conquerors!"

Bouncing back and forth between the living room and den, I did my best, even grabbing low-carb bars off the kitchen counter and waving them in the air. Still, neither of them moved an inch. They knew my game, and I knew theirs.

About that time, Nick came in from his afternoon ride. He'd already been training for months for his next Cape Epic race, and our new eating plan had all started with him.

"What's wrong with the girls?" he asked after glancing between the two rooms.

"Oh," I raised my voice just a tad, "they're just resting up before they dive into their homework. They've had a really big day."

The groans of protest that followed let me know they heard me loud and clear. We really were in it to win it. Hopefully.

Our change in diet had started out as a show of solidarity for Nick. Only a few days before, we'd gone out to dinner and talked about the way he was going to start eating—a diet of low carbs, high protein, and an increase in healthy fats—as part of his training regimen. Overall, we have always been a health-conscious family, but to join him meant taking our awareness to a whole new level. At the time, it seemed the right thing to do. We wanted him to succeed. The more we talked at dinner, the more we convinced ourselves that we could do this. We could eat a little more of some things and a lot less of others. How hard could it be? We'd support Nick and get even more healthy at the same time. It was the perfect plan.

By the time we got home, we were all stoked and on board and immediately set out to put everything that Nick explained was off-limits onto the kitchen island. As we pulled items out of the fridge and out of the pantry, I think we were all a bit shocked to realize what the girls in particular had been eating. They had been convinced they were healthy eaters—and to be honest, I thought so too—but the bags and boxes on the counter told a different story. In their defense, I did recognize that many of the items were leftover snacks from birthday parties or team dinners, but someone was clearly eating what remained. As I picked up a few of the boxes, the ingredients listed on many of them exposed loads of everything we thought none of us were eating. We joked that it exposed the girls' sugar addiction, their bread addiction, their gluten addiction, and, of course, their Goldfish addiction. We all agreed that the Goldfish were definitely not there by accident.

Taking it all in, I couldn't help but wonder, *How did we get here?* It obviously had happened gradually, without any of us really noticing. At some point, the girls had just drifted away from healthy eating. With them becoming teenagers and us living on the go even more, it was probably easier to do than any of us thought. With all their friends and our team in and out of the house for one get-together or another, the stockpiling of unhealthy carbs and sugar-laden foods had gone undetected. If only we'd been inspired to do this much sooner. It was definitely time for a reset.

On the first day, the girls had been a bit moody, but still totally on board.

On the second day, I could hear little grumblings—and not just their stomachs.

By the third day, mutiny was brewing. Catherine was convinced she had all the flu-like symptoms you can actually develop. To my surprise, she really had googled it. I had no idea that such a thing was even a thing, but it was. I guess when you detox from anything, you feel worse before you get better, but it's always worth it, right? At least that's what I was trying to convince my girls.

I knew this was going to be just as good for me as it was for Nick and his training goals—and our girls. Pushing the pause button and resetting certain aspects of our lives is always a good thing. Maybe this would be when God delivered me from my genetically inspired love for bread!

You see, for Greek people, no meal is complete without bread, whether it's traditional, cheesy, divinely olive, or laden with raisins. To serve a meal without bread would be like eating a Greek salad without olives or feta cheese.[1] If you did, it just wouldn't be a Greek salad. It would be lettuce tossed with a few vegetables and olive oil. A meal without bread is unthinkable. If you asked Mum about it, she'd probably say that if Jesus is the Bread of Life, then a low-carb diet can't possibly be from God (John 6:35). Even when we had communion at church growing up, it was from two well-kneaded loaves representing both the divine and human natures of Jesus, and each loaf was

> Pushing the pause button and resetting certain things in our lives is always a good thing.

stamped with a seal of many pictures embedded in a shape like a cross.[2] *Prosforo*, we called it, and there were women who baked it all fifty-two weeks of the year. It was part of their service to the church. So even thinking about forgoing bread was almost sacrilegious to my Greek sensibilities, and thus to my family as well. But we had decided to do it together, and so we soldiered on.

By the time Team Caine made it to the thirty-day mark—and miraculously, we did—our eating habit transformation was complete. We all regained some much-needed awareness of what we were putting in our mouths, and our girls began to actually want the healthier choices. To watch them reach for a piece of fruit or a handful of nuts for a snack made supporting Nick and his goals more than worth it. We weren't going to eat keto forever, but supporting Nick and course-correcting some of our eating habits at the same time had turned out to be a really good move. (And might I add right here that by telling you of our experience, I am in no way endorsing a keto diet. I strongly caution you, if you're interested in trying it, to check with your doctor first. We did it for a short period of time for a specific purpose.)

From the start, the spiritual implications of our journey were never lost on me. We were being transformed physically, from the inside out, but it took a rather drastic external change to begin a massive internal reset of our systems—and to get us into ketosis. But once that internal reset happened, we began to feel healthier. We had more energy, we had more focus, and we were more effective overall. Sometimes, spiritually, I think we need to do the same. We need to do something fairly drastic externally in order to reset ourselves internally. We need to implement a change, maybe cut something out of our lives. We need to stop doing one thing so we can start doing something else—all for the purpose of stopping ourselves from drifting and then kick-starting our spiritual hunger and passion in some specific area.

Maybe some of us feel bored, like life has gone flat. Maybe we're spiraling out of control, barely hanging on by a thread, wondering how we ever got to where we are. Sometimes, maybe more times than we'd like, we find ourselves in a place wondering how we can feel so far from the One who said he'd never leave us or forsake us (Deut. 31:6, 8; Josh. 1:5; Heb. 13:5). The One who is the anchor of our souls (Heb. 6:19). In that place we ask, *Why does it feel like I've drifted so far from my purpose and passion?*

When we feel this way, perhaps, without meaning to, without even realizing it, we have allowed certain heart attitudes, behaviors, habits, or patterns of thinking to become part of our lives—just like all the junk food that crept into my pantry. Maybe it's time for a spiritual clean out. Perhaps we need to go *spiritual keto* in one area or another to stop drifting and to get from where we are to where we were created to be.

Now, before you break out in a cold sweat wondering what you might need to clean out of your spiritual pantry, relax. I'm not going to tell you what you need to radically toss out of your life—that's between you and God—but I am going to tell you what God wants us all to be hungering and thirsting after so that we stay focused, feeding ourselves spiritually nutritious food that will help us keep from drifting and recalibrate us if we have drifted.

SPIRITUAL KETO

Jesus obviously cared a great deal about our spiritual diet. In the Sermon on the Mount, he said, "Blessed are those who hunger and thirst for righteousness, for they shall be satisfied" (Matt. 5:6 ESV). Our appetites matter to God. He knows what will satisfy us the most, what is most nutritious, what will give us spiritual focus, energy, peace, and joy—and right here he tells us that it is righteousness.

I can't help but read this verse and wonder if somewhere along the way, Jesus went spiritual keto on us. I'm sure you won't find such notions in any commentary, but these are the kinds of things that just pop into my mind, especially when I'm in a season of not eating bread . . . freshly baked Greek bread, in particular.

> Our appetites matter to God. He knows what will satisfy us the most, what is most nutritious, what will give us spiritual focus, energy, peace, and joy.

Seriously, though, how exactly do you hunger and thirst for righteousness? Do you mix it, knead it, and bake it? Do you whip it up and refrigerate it? Or throw it in a blender and drink it like a shake? When I have questions, I do what you do—I google it. Well, okay, when it's spiritual, I admit that I do a lot more biblical and theological research. And I pray. Aren't you glad? Anyway, here is some of what I've learned about this.

Let's start with some foundation setting. What is righteousness? *Righteousness* is not a word we use in our everyday language, but it communicates a powerful biblical truth. *Righteousness* is right standing before God. It's a free gift, just like our salvation, and it's what we are made to be when we accept Christ. Paul wrote to the Corinthians, saying that God "made the one who did not know sin to be sin for us, so that in him we might become the righteousness of God" (2 Cor. 5:21).

Being righteous is standing before God blameless. Can you imagine? Utterly blameless! When God looks at us, he sees us as righteous because he sees us through the finished work of what Jesus did for us on the cross. Jesus became our sin so that we could become his righteousness. What an incredible exchange.

I realize this idea of righteousness being so freely given can be hard to grasp, particularly because we're so conditioned to earn most things that we receive—grades, awards, privileges, promotions, paychecks, opportunities, approval, and on the list could go. Virtually everything surrounding our lives is awarded to us based on our behavior, on our working for it to prove our worthiness. But God *made* us righteous (2 Cor. 5:21), and it is one of the greatest gifts he has given to us, because it's based on what Jesus did, not on anything that we have done or ever could do. In fact, when Paul wrote to the Romans, he said, "There is no one righteous, not even one" (3:10). Not one includes you and me—and everyone else we know.

When I first gave my heart fully to Christ, I came from such a broken background full of sin and shame that it was hard for me to comprehend I was the righteousness of God. Even though my head knew that I had been declared righteous because of the atoning work of Jesus on the cross, I felt nothing but unrighteous and ashamed. Maybe that's how you feel too. I remember spending weeks and months, even years, doing my best to renew the way I thought and felt. So many times, I would just say aloud or under my breath, "I am the righteousness of God in Christ Jesus." I wrote it in my journal. I noted it in the margin of my Bible. I placed it on sticky notes. I did everything I could to get that pivotal truth off the pages of my Bible and into my heart. Gradually, it happened, but to this day, I need to regularly declare this truth to myself.

When I remember who I am in Christ, I want the things that a righteous person wants, and I tend to act more like a righteous person would. I think, speak, or act like who I really am. But when I forget who I am, I start drifting, and I tend to think, speak, and act like the person I used to be when I was not in Christ. I end up feeding my flesh instead of my spirit, and my diet is exposed in my external words and deeds. In the end, I don't reflect the fruit of the Spirit that I truly want to—love, joy, peace, patience, kindness, goodness, faithfulness, gentleness, and self-control.

No doubt, there is a direct correlation between knowing who I am and the things I hunger and thirst after and how I subsequently behave. If I try hard enough in my own natural willpower, I can easily act like a righteous person—say for about five minutes—but I cannot live consistently like who I am without truly knowing and believing that I am the righteousness of God in Christ Jesus.

When Jesus walked this earth, his mission was to fulfill God's righteousness (Matt. 3:15). By coming to earth, he brought the work of the kingdom and the gift of salvation to us (Rom. 6:23). And in his teachings, he made it clear that righteousness is an outflow from a life in him that is centered on submitting, worshipping, and seeking after our heavenly Father. In the sections of Scripture following his Sermon on the Mount, over the course of three chapters, Jesus addressed the moral substance of righteous living—the outflow of what a life in him should look like. In Matthew 5 he said:

- We are to be salt and light in the world (vv. 13–16).
- We are to keep our oaths to God and not let murder or adultery enter our hearts (vv. 17–32).

- We're to go the extra mile, tell the truth, and love our enemies (vv. 33–48).
- In chapter 6 he told us how to give, how to pray, and how to fast (vv. 1–18). He told us how to steward our possessions and overcome anxiety (vv. 19–34). And he finished the lesson in chapter 7 when he told us not to judge, how to ask him for what we need, and how to build our lives on the right foundation.

The rest of the Gospels and New Testament are, of course, also filled with verses that teach us how to live in right relationship with God and with one another; nowhere does God tell us that our Christian walk is to be lived out of a life steeped in duty and obligation. Rather, we are to live with our lives fully and freely yielded to him.

When we drift, however, our appetite for righteousness wanes, and then we naturally try to satisfy our hunger with things that will never satisfy, just as we do physically when we fill up our tanks on sugar and empty carbs. We're hungry, but for the wrong kinds of foods, and what we reach for tastes good, though it might not be what is the absolute best for us.

So how do we hunger and thirst for righteousness and nothing else? After all, righteousness is not bread. It's not baklava. It's not anything we can touch, taste, feel, or eat. Or is it?

PURSUE RIGHTEOUSNESS

While you may not know where I'm going with this chapter, all this talk about righteousness and righteous living may have you breaking out in hives. I totally get it, especially if you come from any kind of legalistic background. In fact, you may have intentionally drifted and cut yourself off from anything to do with Christianity because all you ever heard was "Don't do this, don't touch that, don't watch that, don't go there, don't speak like that, don't dress like that, don't feel that way." It's hard to love Jesus and hunger after his righteousness when the dos and don'ts seem to contradict much of what he came to give us. I can almost hear some of the things you might have said before you drifted away: "The Christian life was supposed to be an abundant life. Where is the abundance in all the don'ts? Where is the life? Where is the joy? Where is the peace? Where's the love?" Even now, as you see the word *righteous* in print, it may be hard not to have a visceral reaction. You want to shut this book, throw it against the wall, or use it as a doorstop.

I get it, but stay with me. Take a deep breath. I'm not going to tell you what you can and can't do. I'm not your mother, though you might think of me that way spiritually. If you do, I'm honored, but like I said earlier, I'm not about to tell you what to clean out of your spiritual pantry. Yes, you might need to go keto in some area of your spiritual life, but I trust God will show that to you. I just want to help you identify if you've stopped hungering and thirsting after righteousness and, therefore, have drifted from Jesus. I want to help you before you land in a place you didn't expect and find yourself asking, *How did I get here?*

Now, if you are already there, I want you to know that you can always find your way back. Jesus will walk on water to come and get you. He loves you that much and more. You are not too far gone. It's not too late. Not ever.

Sometimes, I think we get saved and enthusiastically hunger

after righteousness, but when we find ourselves inundated by all the dos and don'ts, we start to drift—and understandably so. Who wants all the love that first envelops us to be turned into rules and regulations? Especially when most of them are too hard to keep in our own strength. Who wants all the beauty of first finding Christ to be soured by chronic feelings of falling short? None of us, I feel sure. All those dos and don'ts just lead to feelings of guilt, anxiousness, shame, condemnation, and failure—none of which God ever intended for us. He pursued us because he loves us and wants to walk in fellowship with us. He wants us to have an abundantly fruitful life. In return, he wants us to pursue him.

To find God and then continue to hunger and thirst after him even though we couldn't have found God at all if he hadn't pursued us first is the necessary paradox of our Christian walk. Jesus said, "No one can come to me unless the Father who sent me draws him" (John 6:44). It's like a cycle that's supposed to be perpetual: First, God draws us to him. Second, we accept him. Third, we pursue him. Fourth, we keep pursuing him. All the days of our lives. We hunger and thirst after righteousness. We get to know him, and we keep going for more.

And yet, it's all too easy to fall into the idea that if we've found him, we need no longer seek him—but that's not how we keep from drifting. The day we stop seeking is the day we start drifting. Perhaps that is why Jesus exhorted the disciples to "seek first the kingdom of God and his righteousness, and all these things will be provided for you" (Matt. 6:33). *Seek* in the Greek is *zēteō*. In a literal sense it means "to search, to strive, to extend great effort to find or accomplish something."[3]

Jesus himself commands us to extend great effort to pursue the kingdom of God *and* his righteousness first. We will talk more about the kingdom of God in the next chapter, but notice here the word *and*. The kingdom of God is not separated from righteousness, but we are supposed to pursue *both* the kingdom of God *and* righteousness *first*. God cares about both. We tend to emphasize one or the other, but both matter to God. I understand that we live in a day of many distractions. I know how easy it is for my own pursuit of righteousness to fall into second, third, or fourth place. I can easily get sidetracked by my own feelings, opinions, desires, and wants, but Jesus gives us a powerful key to keep from drifting, and that is to pursue the kingdom *and* his righteousness first.

How many times do we end up thinking, doing, or saying what is completely unrighteous, all because our pursuit of righteousness slipped from first place? I have found over and over that when I put first things first, everything else tends to fall into place.

When Paul wrote to his protégé, Timothy, he said we're to be vessels of honor, sanctified, useful to God, and prepared for every good work. Then he went on to say, "Flee from youthful passions, and pursue righteousness, faith, love, and peace, along with those who call on the Lord from a pure heart" (2 Tim. 2:21–22). It's interesting to me that Paul went from telling Timothy to flee youthful passions to telling him to pursue righteousness. Most of us have heard about fleeing. We're quite familiar with all the things we need to run away from—you know, the list of dos and don'ts—but are we as familiar with what we should be pursuing?

When my girls were young and I'd tell them not to go toward something that was dangerous, like the street out in front of our house, invariably when I turned my back, that was the one thing they wanted to run for. It seemed like my saying it was off-limits is what attracted them to want to experience it. They were normal children! I had to learn what most mothers do and give them something far more interesting to think about, to focus on, to pursue. Diverting their attention was the best way to keep them safe—all the while teaching them what was best for them.

In the same way, God says "don't" because he knows that very thing we're tempted to reach for will jeopardize our flourishing. When God says no, it is not because he is trying to withhold anything good from us; it's because he's trying to get something even better to us. Every one of God's limits is an act of profound love. He's looking out for us! His gifts are good! For every good and perfect gift is from God, and no good thing does he withhold from those who live in integrity (James 1:17; Ps. 84:11). God's dos and don'ts are for our best. They are not designed to hurt or harm us. What we have to learn is to trust him and flee from the destructive things—even when they feel right and good to our flesh—so we can run toward Jesus and his righteousness.

If we'll take our focus off changing our behavior and then fix our eyes on Jesus (Heb. 12:2), running hard after him, righteousness will change us—instead of us trying to change ourselves. It will anchor us in Jesus and help us not drift with the currents of the day and the age in which we live.

It's just like going keto. When our family started fleeing sugar and flour and unhealthy carbohydrates, we started pursuing healthier choices. We ran for the good stuff. And eventually we quit wanting the bad stuff. Sometimes the easiest way to solve a problem is to pursue the solution.

> Sometimes the easiest way to solve a problem is to pursue the solution.
> And the solution for our souls is the anchor of our souls: Jesus.

And the solution for our souls is the anchor of our souls: Jesus. See, running away from our youthful passions—whatever they may be—and running to Jesus is running to life. Do you know why? Because Jesus doesn't just give us life—although he does do that, and the life he gives us is life more abundant—he is life! He is the way, the truth, and the life (John 14:6). He's the resurrection and the life (John 11:25). To receive Jesus is to receive life. Life is not just a gift he gives us; it's who he is. To run to him is to run to life.

But even if we understand that, it still leaves a few questions unanswered. How do we pursue righteousness? How do we hunger? How do we thirst?

HOW DO WE HUNGER?

To start, we hunger by hungering. (I know, that sounds simplistic . . . hang with me.) Hunger starts with longing for more of God. So often we get complacent in our pursuit of God because we believe we already have all of God that there is to have. Now, of course, we don't say it aloud, but our actions speak for themselves. Why pursue what we already possess? Our lack of pursuit reveals that we believe we already have what we want.

But there is always more of God to be had. Always. For you and for me. Do you realize that no matter how long or how far we run after God, we will never exhaust him? We will never get to his end. He is inexhaustible. We can know him and still have so much to know about the depth of his riches (Rom. 11:33). We can know his love and still have so much to know of the width, length, height, and depth of his love (Eph. 3:18). We can know his mercy and still experience his mercy new every day (Lam. 3:22–23). We can hear from him and still have so much more to hear from him.

We start hungering by hungering. By wanting more of him. By asking for more of him. If you realize that you lack hunger, then ask him to grow it. He will. He is faithful. He loves to answer a prayer for more of him.

We start hungering by asking, but don't stop there. Follow asking with feasting. As we have already talked about, we crave what we eat. What is your daily diet—spiritually? Are you feasting daily on the Bread of Life? Are you taking the time to be with God, in his Word and in prayer every day? So many people have such a strong start in their walk with Christ, implementing these practices and growing as they do, but then at some point, they come to believe they have grown beyond these practices—and then they stop growing as they stop feasting. Time with God is not elemental but essential. Essential for growing in him, growing with him, and growing in his righteousness. As we spend time with God, he changes us. He grows us. He grows our desire for more of him. He grows our hunger and thirst—our desire— for righteousness.

Pursuing righteousness requires feasting, but it also requires fasting. Like our stomachs, our hearts have only so much space. Our minds have only so much space. Our souls have only so much space. In order to feast we have to fast. We have to make space for more.

All through the years, it has been my practice to step back and evaluate what I'm spending my time pursuing—in case I've drifted and my priorities have gotten out of alignment. There have been times when I've chosen to fast from things to stay close to Jesus. Sometimes it was food or TV, sometimes certain friends or books, and other times the news or social media. Usually just simple things. And it was often for a season, not forever.

That's how it was when our family cut out the unhealthy carbs. We weren't planning on never eating carbs again. I'm not sure the girls would have ever survived that, but when we realized how much they had gotten off track, it became a necessary step. I have found that some things need to leave our lives for good—because they truly are detrimental to us—and some just need to leave for a period of time, until we can get ourselves firmly anchored once more. In other words, some of us can eat one slice of pizza, and some of us can't help but eat the whole pizza. I won't say which one I am, but suffice it to say, it's better that I not eat pizza too often.

Are you hungering and thirsting for righteousness, for more of him? You know by what you want, by what you feast on, and by what you fast from. Are you feasting on him and fasting from what causes you to drift? Or are you fasting from him and feasting on what causes you to drift? If you have drifted, maybe it's time to go keto—spiritually. Maybe it's time to make a change—even a drastic one—not for legalistic reasons but in order to stop drifting, get anchored in Jesus once more, and pursue righteousness again.

I don't know what you're hungering and thirsting for right now, but the good news is that you won't have to give up carbs; you will get to feast on the Bread of Life. Trust me, it's never too late to change your eating habits. To go from junk food to healthy food. To go from gorging on the world to hungering after God. To hungering and thirsting after righteousness. To pursuing righteousness with all your heart.

8

YOU STOP WORKING AND
YOU START WATCHING

Do all the good you can, by all the means you can, in
all the ways you can, in all the places you can, at all
the times you can, to all the people you can, as long as
ever you can.

—JOHN WESLEY'S RULE

Staring out the kitchen window at the men working in our
backyard, all I could do was shake my head. Mum was at it
again. It seemed she lived through every winter for this annual
spring ritual. This moment of conquest. This testament to our
Greekness.

I braced myself for what I knew would come next, for what

I had come to dread in recent years. It didn't matter that I had loads of homework or was in my last year of high school or that I felt too old to indulge Mum and her crazy Greek and sentimental ways. She would ask—and her ask was never an ask.

"Christina, the men will be ready for you soon," she started. "Take your shoes off and wash your feet. This time, I want imprints of your hands and your feet."

I wanted to protest, but I didn't dare. All my life I had been taught why this was so important. To Mum. To our ancestors. To all the dead Greeks we'd never met. I could feel the pressure of history bearing down on me. How many times had my dad reminded me that three centuries before the Romans perfected it, the Greeks invented modern-day concrete?[1] Yes, the Egyptians used a form of mortar or early cement in building the pyramids, but no mind.[2] To a Greek, that didn't count. It was just the pyramids, and the mortar they used wasn't exactly the same as concrete—and if the Greeks could take credit for something, they most definitely would. Consequently, concrete to a Greek carried as much national pride as the Olympics, and to Mum, we had an obligation to carry the torch. I was convinced that she was on a personal mission to carry the legacy of concrete as far as she could pay to have it poured.

Little by little, year after year, she worked to save money and hire a crew to cover our backyard. Section by section. Plot by plot. And she wanted the hands and feet of us three kids to time stamp each of her property annexations. Do you have any idea how embarrassing it is to be a teenager and have some strange man guide your foot onto wet concrete? I wasn't sure how many more years Mum would require this, but I was beginning to want the entire yard covered far more quickly than she did.

At the time, and despite its small geographical footprint, Greece was leading Europe and the Americas in concrete production. They had even begun bagging it and shipping it.[3] I feel sure, if it had been cost effective, Mum would have loved nothing better than to have her concrete imported from the motherland, though I'm not sure it would have looked any different. After all, gray is gray, right? Of course, Greece no longer holds such a prestigious position in the world of concrete production, but I surmise it's only because of simple supply and demand. I imagine there's probably very little grass left in Greece, thanks to national pride and people like Mum.

I'll always believe that Mum got each section of concrete poured at the beginning of summer, not just because she'd saved money all winter but also because that gave her the rest of the summer to hose it off. Whether it needed it or not. As long as the weather was warm, if Mum went missing, we knew to first look in the backyard—and there she'd be, hosing the concrete, pushing all the little leaves and debris from the tree to the back edge of the slab. For hours at a time. You see, to a Greek, a hose is a broom. In fact, it's sometimes referred to as a Greek broom.[4] Or a Mediterranean broom.[5] And no matter how many strides conservationists make teaching us to conserve water, a true Greek hoses away. I'm not saying it's right or good for the planet or even fiscally responsible, but that's the way it was—especially for Mum.

My parents and all their friends used to say that if you wanted the property values to go up in a neighborhood, then invite the Greeks to move in, because no one knows how to pour a slab like a Greek. And no one knows how to use a Greek broom like a Greek. Spoofing Julius Caesar who said, *"Veni, vidi, vici,"* meaning, "I came; I saw; I conquered," I can still hear them laughing and shouting, "We came! We saw! We concreted!"

They were so proud of their crazy Greek ways. Sometimes, despite all the stories of how they came to Sydney and left everything behind, I felt sure they left nothing behind—because they brought all their Greekness with them. Including their penchant to pour concrete on every square inch of real estate possible. By the time I was grown, our backyard was the perfect setting for fifty people dancing like Zorba the Greek or two teams of full-court basketball. Take your pick.

To be honest, everything about our lives saluted our heritage—not just our concrete slab of a yard. Our entire home—along with plenty others—had more trinkets and statues and tributes to the motherland than you could imagine. Even the fronts of our homes often gave away the shrine that lay just beyond the front door. If something could be painted, bought, or displayed in blue and white colors, it was. Everything from Ionic columns to painted porch furniture to flowerpots saluted Greece. Trust me, if someone had been building and selling backyard sheds styled after the Parthenon, then I feel sure my parents and every one of their friends would have bought one—but only after they poured another section of concrete on which to set it.

Because my parents—and all their friends—immigrated to Australia with no one to rely on but one another, this is just the way they were. They looked to one another for everything. From where to buy a car to where to find a job to whom you should hire for your concrete work. They huddled together, firmly entrenched in the idea that there was safety in numbers, even long after they were settled and it really wasn't necessary. Looking back, I can understand their fear of the unknown, but growing up the daughter of first-generation Greek immigrants definitely meant growing up in a very Greek bubble.

All my childhood, I lived inside that bubble. I remember one time in elementary school when I was invited to a sleepover at a school friend's house, Mum said no, just because she wasn't Greek. I'm not sure anything made my parents feel more threatened than non-Greeks and their ways, so all my life, if I were allowed to go to a birthday party, it was because it was an all-Greek party. If our family went to a wedding, it was because it was an all-Greek wedding. If we went to any kind of event, it was because it was within our tight-knit Greek community. But the older I grew, the harder it was for me to understand why my parents and aunts and uncles and cousins and all their Greek friends and neighbors stayed to themselves as much as possible, as though they were afraid of what might happen if they ventured out into a culture that wasn't their own. They trusted no one but each other. And it wasn't because they didn't speak English. My parents actually spoke five languages. In addition to the Arabic they learned from growing up in Egypt, they spoke Greek, French, Italian, and English. They were brilliant people! They knew how to navigate modern society, but they chose to live in a small world of their own making.

For me and my brothers, all of this homogeneous living was just the way it was—and I think my parents truly expected us to carry on our Greek heritage as though the rest of Sydney's cultural diversity and influence didn't exist. But we weren't them.

We were Australians—by birth. We wanted to explore our country and all it had to offer. I loved eating my feta cheese and olive sandwiches, but I was equally curious about my non-Greek friends and their lunches of white bread and Vegemite paste— something I grew to love and still enjoy to this day. For as long as

I can remember, I wanted to venture out. I wanted to know how other people lived, what they ate, and what they talked about. I wanted to know what they did for fun, what they celebrated, even what they thought. I wanted to break out of the bubble. And I suppose, in my own way, I did. Little by little.

All through the years of growing up, I pushed the envelope. Especially for a girl. I was studious. I was an independent thinker. I was a leader. Even when it got me into trouble. Which was most of the time. In our world, a girl was never encouraged to be bookish or intellectual or to have any aspirations other than to marry and have children. I did want to marry and have children, but I also had a sense that there was more I was called to do—though I didn't have any idea what that might be. And unlike most of my family, I was willing to risk finding out. Surely there were other possibilities. I seemed to have a mind of my own from the start, which, admittedly, made me a bubble-breaker from the start.

Of all the little ways I caused a rumble, my decision to attend the University of Sydney was one of the biggest. When I surrendered my life fully to the lordship of Jesus at twenty-one, it was an even bigger move. When I started going to a different church regularly at twenty-two and then enrolled in Bible school and later stepped into ministry, my family wasn't even sure who I was anymore. And understandably so, because no one in my family had ever done any of that. I had stepped so far out of the safe, insular Greek bubble they had created, and away from all their expectations for me, that they thought they had lost me for life. If only they had understood that leaving the bubble never meant abandoning who I was, but it meant embracing more of who I was created to be.

THE NATURE OF BUBBLES

Now that I've lived outside the bubble for more than thirty years, I've come to understand quite a lot about bubbles—especially that they can be built for as many reasons, it seems, as there are people. They can come in all shapes and sizes. They can exist in any part of the world and in any segment of society. They can be family ones. Cultural ones. Educational ones. Career ones. Economic ones. National ones. Religious ones. Political ones. They can be related to age or ethnicity or gender. They can be built around an ideology, a set of values or goals, a passion or pursuit. Bubbles can be built to keep people in or to keep people out. They can be built for good reasons and to do good things. Conversely, they can be built for bad reasons and to promote bad things. But no matter how or why a bubble might exist, it's still a bubble, and therein lies the problem.

The challenge with bubbles is they can limit us in so many ways. They carry the potential to curb our experiences, influence, creativity, and even our worldviews. They can limit our understanding, tolerance, and empathy, especially when it comes to those living outside our particular bubble. And yet, no matter how constricting they are, it seems so much easier to live inside a bubble than outside one.

Of all the bubbles I've observed through the years, there's one in particular that we Christ followers should be vigilant about. If we're not careful, we

> If we're not careful, we can inadvertently settle for a Christian lifestyle that restricts us to living inside the bubble of the Christian subculture—instead of living the abundant life Jesus called us to live out in the real, live world.

can inadvertently settle for a Christian lifestyle that restricts us to living inside the bubble of the Christian subculture—instead of living the abundant life Jesus called us to live out in the real, live world.

I understand that living in the Christian bubble can be alluring. That it can just happen. There is great comfort, familiarity, and safety in having only Christian friends and moderating ourselves to only seeing Christian movies, reading Christian books, and listening to Christian podcasts. There's a security and an ease in attending church, Bible studies, retreats, and conferences with other Christians. Once we learn the language, understand the dynamics, and find our rhythm, we can spend all our time in the bubble, never venturing out. And that's when we can forget that Jesus told us, "Go, therefore, and make disciples of all nations, baptizing them in the name of the Father and of the Son and of the Holy Spirit" (Matt. 28:19) and "Go into all the world and preach the gospel to all creation" (Mark 16:15).

Do you notice that he said to go into all the world, not into all the Christian bubbles and hide until he returns? Why would Jesus tell us to go into all the world? Because *"God [so] loved the world . . .* he gave his one and only Son, so that everyone who believes in him will not perish but have eternal life" (John 3:16, emphasis mine).

I understand how easy it might be to look around at the chaos in our world and think God must just be waiting to blow it up and start again—that he hates the world and how messed up it has become—but nothing could be further from the truth. God loves the world, so much so that he sent Jesus to the world, and then Jesus sent us. Even on the last night of his life, before he was crucified, he prayed for himself to be glorified, he prayed for his disciples, and he prayed for us (John 17).

Just as last words are so important, so are final prayers. And this is what Jesus prayed: "My prayer is *not* that you take them out of the world but that you protect them from the evil one. They are not of the world, even as I am not of it. Sanctify them by the truth; your word is truth. As you sent me into the world, *I have sent them into the world*" (vv. 15–18 NIV, emphasis mine).

Even though Jesus prayed that God would not take us out of the world, sometimes, without meaning to, we do this ourselves . . . typically because we've taken the bait of one of three foes. Three foes that result in mission drift.

THE BUBBLE . . . AND THE PRESENCE OF FEAR

I can't help but remember all the times my mother tried to keep me inside the Greek bubble. Because she didn't understand the Australian people and culture, she feared the unknown. Instead of trying to understand Australian culture, we were taught to avoid assimilating with it, so as not to lose any of our Greekness. She was trying to protect me because she thought that if I ventured outside the bubble, then I most assuredly would be corrupted, lose my values, abandon our culture, and forsake our traditions. But I was being suffocated by the bubble, because I was never created to live in a bubble—be it Greek or any other kind. And neither were you.

Sometimes I think we fear being tarnished by people who are not Christians—if not in reality, then possibly in reputation. The latter was the primary fear of most of the religious leaders of Jesus' day. They

> I was never created to live in a bubble— be it Greek or any other kind. And neither were you.

fretted about their appearance; they cared more about being seen as holy than actually being holy, wholly devoted to God and his mission. They criticized and critiqued Jesus for the company he kept—sinners and tax collectors. And what did Jesus do in response? He said to them, "Those who are well have no need of a physician, but those who are sick. I came not to call the righteous, but sinners" (Mark 2:17 ESV).

When we first come to Christ, we may need to step away from certain settings—to turn from strongholds of sin—while we take new steps of growth in him. And even after we continue to mature in him, we need to be wise and prayerful about not placing ourselves in situations and settings that tempt us.

But that wisdom is much different than living as a captive to fear and a Christian who is off mission. When we bow to fear—not wisdom—and refuse to step out of our bubbles because of the risk of "contamination," we make a statement: that we believe the Holy Spirit of God who lives on the inside of us—you know, the same Spirit who raised Jesus from the dead—is not powerful enough to keep us from becoming worldly even while being in the world. But that is one of the reasons Jesus sent the Holy Spirit to live in us: he gives us the power to be witnesses *in the world* (Acts 1:8). We have the power to be in the world and not of it because the Holy Spirit dwells in us, and we've been commissioned to go into all the world.

THE BUBBLE ... AND THE LOSS OF FOCUS

A second foe of mission is a loss of focus. Sometimes we stay in the bubble because we can't see past the bubble. Because we have become shortsighted in our vision. Because we have replaced his mission with another: the mission of *go* with the mission of *stay*.

When we replace our call to follow Jesus into all the world to make disciples with a call to solely learn how to live a good, moral life in the Christian bubble—merely trying not to sin until we die and go to heaven where everything will be awesome—we grow bored, frustrated, and weary. Why? Because we are not flourishing in the very place Jesus has called us to be, which is in the world.

When we lose focus and exchange his mission for another, we miss out on all the adventure and purpose God has planned for us here on earth. Deep down, we feel untethered from Jesus and his purpose because we yearn to do what we were created to do. Go. Into all the world. And make disciples. Since we're not doing what we were created to do, we're drifting—further and further from the purpose he put us on the planet for.

Now, I'm not suggesting that we run away from our Christian communities and exchange them for living in the world altogether. As we've already discovered, the practices of praying, going to the Word, gathering together, and walking in greater holiness are essential to keeping us anchored to Jesus. But if we are not deliberate in taking all that we learn and grow into through our Christian journey out into the world, then we can easily find ourselves drifting in a way we never expected, rarely interacting with non-Christians. We can find ourselves slowly retreating and no longer making the effort to meet new people who do not look like us, act like us, think like us, or believe like us. We can find ourselves living our entire lives in the bubble because we aren't looking beyond the bubble.

THE BUBBLE ... AND THE ABSENCE OF FAITH

When Jesus walked on this earth, the kingdom of God broke into the world in great power. Jesus opened blind eyes (Mark 10:46–52). He healed deaf ears (Mark 7:35). He spoke, and those who were crippled walked (Luke 13:10–17; John 5:1–14). He multiplied food (Matt. 14:13–21). He turned water into wine (John 2:1–12). He commanded the forces of evil to go—and they went (Matt. 8:28–34). He stood up for the downtrodden and against injustice.[6] He advocated for the poor and the exploited (Luke 4:18). It's no wonder he talked about the kingdom more than anything else (Luke 4:43). About changing this world. About bringing heaven to earth. Even when Jesus prayed what we now call the Lord's Prayer, he said, "Your kingdom come. Your will be done on earth as it is in heaven" (Matt. 6:10).

The kingdom of God is defined as "the rule of God." *The rule of God* is *the act of God* to set things right and to help people and the world work as he intended.[7] Therefore, part of our doing the work of the kingdom here on earth means that when we see what's wrong, we do what we can to make it right. When we see poverty, prejudice, sexism, racism, hatred, misogyny, abuse, inequality, joblessness, a lack of access to education or health care, or a lack of creation care, if it is in our power to do something, then we do it. We're called to make barren places fruitful, to bring reconciliation and restoration everywhere we can, to everyone we can.[8]

Imagine the difference we could make in people's lives if every time we saw injustice, we chose to get involved? Wouldn't the people we help be far more open to us and to a God who cares deeply about them and their issues?

Until Jesus comes back a second time to establish his physical kingdom on this earth in full, he wants us doing what he did. He wants us drawing people's attention to God and his goodness, and all the ways he's gracious, merciful, compassionate, and worthy to be trusted. He wants us to understand that we have not only been saved *from* something, but we have also been saved *for* something, and that is the work of the kingdom here on earth (2 Cor. 5:11–21).

But if we're living in a bubble, then we're drifting away from the very place we've been sent and away from the very people we're supposed to be affecting. Without realizing it, from the vantage point of our bubble, we stop working and we start watching. But that's not what we've been called to do. Dare I suggest that although we're the ones called to reach the lost, if we're trapped inside a world of our own making, inside the subculture of our Christian faith, drifting inside a bubble, then maybe we are the ones who are actually lost.

LOST, LIKE A LETTER IN THE MAIL

When I first moved away from Australia, I missed my mum terribly. I missed running over to her house and dropping something off or picking something up. I missed her hugs, her cooking, and all her updates on the neighbors. I even missed her crazy concrete-hosing ways. She was such an integral part of our lives. Though we lived on the go like any family, we saw her regularly. There was nothing she loved better than to greet my girls as they came bounding through her front door. Like she did with all her grandchildren, she adored them. You can imagine how hard it was to leave her, especially knowing that Catherine and Sophia wouldn't get to continue seeing her as often as they always had. And she wouldn't get to continue seeing them grow up, going to their school activities or events, coming to their birthday parties. It was quite a transition.

I made every effort to call her frequently, but because of the time difference and our busy schedules, it could sometimes be challenging to connect. When I had a little bit of free time because I was sitting in an airport waiting for a flight, I would have to check the day and time before I called. And if she was at one of her regularly scheduled events, such as bingo night— something no one could ever interrupt—then I would have to skip calling.

On several occasions, when we would go for a visit, I would suggest emailing or FaceTiming or texting to keep up on a more regular basis. All she would do was look at me as if I was from Mars. She was terrified of all our modern communication methods. Even when my girls or my nieces and nephews would try to help her text or show her how easy it was to download apps on their own phones, they had great fun and loads of laughs, but the objective of communication was totally unsuccessful. With their help, she could make the attempt, but without them right beside her, it was a no-go. She had mastered the television remote and the telephone on the wall, and that was as far as her techie skills were ever going to go.

So I eventually resorted to one of the oldest methods of communication possible. No, not smoke signals or cave drawings—letters. Yes, I went back to the ancient times before phones and internet and took the time to write my mother letters.

For a woman more given to texts and tweets, it felt like my

world came to a screeching halt every time I picked up a pen to write. But if I wanted to love my mother in the world where she was, then it was letters I would have to write. And though it never seemed to bother her, because of the distance between us, by the time Mum got my letters, at least a week had passed. Our whole family would have lived at least seven more days of adventure, and Mum would just be finding out Catherine had performed in a recital. Or Sophia had finally mastered how to ride a bike. Can you even remember what was in the news a week ago? And sometimes the letters were lost in the mail, and she never received them at all.

To be sure she knew I had written, I would call and say, "Mum, did you get the letter I sent you?"

Most of the time she had. But on some occasions, surprisingly, she would say, "No, Christina, I didn't get it."

Then, of course, I was quick to say, "Well, Mum, I'm sorry. The letter must have gotten lost."

It was so disappointing to learn that Mum never got the letter I sent, so on the phone I would have to recap what I had included in the letter. I'd have to catch her up on all the latest news.

When was the last time you wrote a letter and sent it to someone? Did they get it? Or did it get lost in the mail? Was it a birthday card, an anniversary card, or a thank-you note? I find it interesting that of the many things God compares us to in his Word, one is a letter—and yet it makes perfect sense. Letters are sent, just like we are. The apostle Paul wrote, "You yourselves are our letter, written on our hearts, known and read by everyone. You show that you are Christ's letter, delivered by us, not written with ink but with the Spirit of the living God—not on tablets of stone but on tablets of human hearts" (2 Cor. 3:2–3).

Letters are sent from one place in the world to another. Letters carry messages from one person to another person. They become connections we cherish, remembrances we keep. After Mum passed away a few years ago, and we cleaned out her house, it was so moving to me to find so many of my letters stuffed in drawers in her bedroom and in boxes in her closet. It was as though she kept them close so she could read them again and again. These words of love and relationship.

And that's exactly what we are called to be: God's love letter to the world contained in human flesh, in ordinary people like you and me. God didn't send a text or a social media post. No, he sent us—real-life, flawed, and imperfect people—to carry his message. To go and make disciples. Imagine the difference we could make in people's lives if we actually realized that we are a love letter sent from God to them. It would impact every interaction and relationship we have.

Imagine if we started right where we are, spreading . . .

- Love in the midst of indifference.
- Joy in the midst of sorrow.
- Peace in the midst of chaos.
- Patience in the midst of frenzy.
- Kindness in the midst of cruelty.
- Goodness in the midst of selfishness.
- Faithfulness in the midst of carelessness.
- Gentleness in the midst of hardness.

> Imagine the difference we could make in people's lives if we actually realized that we are a love letter sent from God to them.

- Self-control in the midst of a world spiraling out of control. (Gal. 5:22–23)

The very idea that we are a letter, entrusted with a message, sent to a broken and dying world, is very telling of God, since sending is such a part of who he is and what he does. First, he sent Jesus into the world. Next, Jesus sent us into the world (John 17:15–18). And then Jesus sent the Holy Spirit to empower us as we go into all the world (John 14:15–31). But what happens when he sends us, yet we never arrive? When his message never gets delivered?

When my letters to Mum failed to arrive, and I would call her to tell her they must be lost in the mail somewhere, I never once said, "Mum, *you* must be lost," because she wasn't the one who was lost.

It's the same with us. If we're living letters sent by God to a broken world, and we never arrive, then aren't we the ones who are lost?

Did you catch that? This is such an important concept that I don't want you to read over it too quickly. Perhaps one of the reasons we find ourselves drifting is because we have lost our mission and purpose. We are God's letter that has become stuck in the Christian bubble or distracted with the demands of this world or preoccupied with religious debates and arguments or possibly we've just been having so much fun that we have not realized we are actually lost.

THE WORLD IS AWAITING OUR ARRIVAL

I know that we often refer to people who aren't yet followers of Christ as "the lost." But no matter how lost they are, if we're not going to them, then we are the ones who are lost. Yes, they're lost spiritually, but we know right where they are physically. They're in the office next to ours. They live across the street. They are our brother or cousin or aunt. Maybe our spouse or son or daughter. None of us have far to go to find any of them. In fact, Jesus said, "Listen to what I'm telling you: Open your eyes and look at the fields, because they are ready for harvest" (John 4:35).

For more than two thousand years, through every century and every generation, there have been fields full of people waiting for us to come to them. What would happen if we started seeing our homes, schools, communities, and places of business as fields? And we went to them?

Jesus said, "The harvest is abundant, but the workers are few. Therefore, pray to the Lord of the harvest to send out workers into his harvest" (Matt. 9:37–38).

Jesus didn't say there was a lack of work, only a lack of workers. Can you see that in our world today? There is no lack of need, people, causes, or information. There is no lack of Christian music, books, Bible studies, or churches. There's just a lack of workers going out into the fields, bringing in the harvest.

I'm a city girl, but I've learned a lot from friends who are farmers, most especially that harvesting fruits, vegetables, or grains involves work that goes on all year long, and not just when it's time to gather in the crop. From repairing equipment, fences, and tractors to preparing the soil, planting, and watering, there are 365 days of the year that harvest is on the mind of the farmer. He prepares for it, waits for it, tends to it, and then he brings it in, only to start all over. It's never-ending work, but the rewards are more than worth it.

In the same way, I imagine God wants us all living with this similar kind of attentiveness, looking for and seeing the lost in the fields around us. He wants us praying for them, encouraging them, and helping them in practical ways.

I think we all intuitively feel that it is right to be doing what Jesus did when he walked the earth. He loved the poor, the ostracized, the oppressed, and the dispossessed. He included those marginalized by society, those considered to have no value. Everywhere he went, he broke down barriers and built a bridge between people and God. He went about doing good. It makes so much sense that he would send us out into the world to do the same. During one of the many times Jesus was teaching his disciples, he said, "You are the salt of the earth. . . . You are the light of the world. . . . Let your light shine before others, so that they may see your good works and give glory to your Father in heaven" (Matt. 5:13–14, 16).

Salt and light are both agents of change. They are catalysts, meaning that, by their very makeup, they can't help but change what they come into contact with. Salt enhances food. It seasons it; it preserves it. Light dispels darkness. It illuminates it; it changes the environment so we can see everything we couldn't see before. We are catalysts like salt and light, called to bring about change in the world around us. In our communities. In our workplaces. In our neighborhoods. In our families. Right where we live. In the lives of the people we run into all the time.

When we go into the fields to bring in the harvest, when we act as salt and light in our world, we can't help but take action. We can't help but do good. "For by grace you have been saved through faith. And this is not your own doing; it is the gift of God, not a result of works, so that no one may boast. For we are his workmanship, created in Christ Jesus for good works, which

God prepared beforehand, that we should walk in them" (Eph. 2:8–10 ESV).

God created us all to do good works, ones he prepared for us long before we were ever born. Ones tailor-made for us and directly tied to our purpose. Something we're to be fulfilling until we take our last breath. When we do those good works and the world sees them, it is God who is glorified. Isn't that what we want more than anything? For God to be glorified? Remember, it was Jesus who said that they would see *our good works and glorify our Father,* who is in heaven.

But if we're not doing what we were created to do, then we can easily find ourselves drifting, wondering, *How did I get here?*

What is it he's calling you to do? Who is it he's calling you to reach with all the gifts, talents, abilities, and knowledge you have?

Is it the adult who never had the chance to learn to read?

Is it the woman recently released from incarceration?

Is it the child in need of a foster home?

Is it the children in your community who go to bed hungry every night?

Is it the widow who can't afford a new roof for her home?

Is it the girl with the unexpected pregnancy who doesn't know where to turn for help?

Is it the woman who lives next door? How can you help her? Of all the people you could have lived next to, it's no accident that you live next door to her.

God has chosen you and me to make him known in this world. Isn't that what he told us in Matthew 28? "Go, therefore, and make disciples of all nations . . ." (v. 19). There is no plan B. We are God's plan A. He is fully aware of our flaws, fears, doubts, and insecurities. He understands that we may feel completely inadequate. After all, how can our minds not be flooded with a myriad of questions in response to this big calling? How can we not break out in a cold sweat when we think about what going into all the world might mean? Still, none of this is a surprise to God, and not one of our limitations daunts him. He knows all the people he wants us to reach. He sees and cares about them just as clearly and as deeply as he sees and cares about us. And so he sends us, flaws and all.

BREAK OUT OF YOUR BUBBLE . . . AND GO

God wants us to embrace our identity in him—as disciples he has sent to the world, as coworkers sent to the harvest, as salt and light, as people who get out of the bubble and do the work of his kingdom. My prayer is that each one of us will never underestimate our identity and our power to effect change in someone else's life. I did once—and I've never forgotten. Since then, I have made it a point to never make the same mistake again.

I was in college at the time, and I made a friend who seemed to have everything going for her. Her name was Deborah. She had good grades, all kinds of opportunities, and never had to worry about money. She was beautiful and confident and seemed to have her whole life together. We would meet up regularly to grab a meal together, study for upcoming tests, or just catch up. We became good friends. So I was understandably worried when she stopped answering my calls and I didn't see her anywhere on campus for days. I didn't know what to do, but my concern kept growing until, three days later, she suddenly resurfaced.

Apparently, she had been at a party that had kept going all

that time, where everyone had been taking drugs to stay awake and continue the party. I'll never forget how she described it to me: "There was so much love. There was so much joy. There was so much peace that I was blown away." Then she pulled out a flower from her pocket. "I loved it so much, Chris, that I didn't want you to miss out on the experience, so I saved you half a tablet."

I tried to keep my cool and politely said no thank you, but I was completely thrown. Her words bothered me at a deep level, and I couldn't stop thinking, *This girl loves you so much that she didn't want you to miss out on the love and joy and peace from a drug. And you, Christine, have the true source of love and joy and peace living inside of you, but you are too embarrassed to talk about Jesus because you think she doesn't need him when, it turns out, the one thing she needs the most is Jesus.*

Afterward, I found an empty room and wept. I made a promise to God that I would never allow anyone's passion about anything—drugs, money, success, or even a cause—to be more passionate than my love for Jesus and my willingness to go into all the world and tell people who he is and what he wants to give them: eternal life.[9]

Why do we easily recognize people with messed-up lives as lost but fail to recognize that those who seem to have it all together are lost too? God wants us to understand that lost people look like all people.

Since that day, I have never forgotten there is a God-shaped vacuum in every human heart that can only be filled with the love, joy, and peace of Christ. But he needs us, his workers, to be willing to go and make disciples. To break out of our Christian bubbles. Jesus doesn't want us drifting with the currents of the world, nor does he want us drifting inside the Christian bubble.

Instead, Jesus wants us to go into the world where he's sent us, anchored in him, to help other people become anchored in him. This was so important to Jesus that after his resurrection, he made sure to give us our "work" before he went to be seated at the right hand of the Father. In fact, they were some of his last words on this earth.

Last words are some of the most important words someone can speak to us, aren't they? I'll always treasure my own mother's last words to me. My brother helped her FaceTime with me, and I remember looking at her sweet smile and hearing her say, "I love you."

Jesus had been away from heaven for thirty-three years, and on his way home, he paused to give us these last words: "Go, therefore, and make disciples . . ." I believe it's time we make Jesus' last command our greatest priority, don't you?

If we are to fulfill our purpose, then we will need to go where we can make disciples—and that will never be at arm's length. I didn't need to go to a party with my friend or accept the pill she offered me, but what I realized those many years ago is that I needed to be salt and light in her world. And if we're going to be the salt and light we've been called to be, then we'll have to get out of the saltshaker. We'll have to get out of our comfort zones and intentionally rub elbows with worldly people. We'll have to break out of our bubbles—and go.

9

YOU STOP PRESSING AND
YOU START COASTING

Our greatest weakness lies in giving up. The most certain
way to succeed is always to try just one more time.

—THOMAS EDISON

There are few things I love more than running along the coast
when the sun is setting. God's brushstrokes across the vast canvas
of the unending sky are always stunning. The swath of colors, the
rays of light, the clouds passing through the moment. The way
the heavens shimmer across the waves of the ocean. It's as though
it was all designed to help me forget that I'm actually gulping for
air, sweating off toxins, and exhausting myself completely.

Today's sky was especially spectacular. It was awash in blues and purples, yellows and brilliant whites. The hues dancing on the water and the sand seemed more vibrant than ever. I was home in California, after a week of travel, and it felt so good to be running on the beach, soaking up as much of God's handiwork as I could. I had started out thinking it would help me to fight a bit of jet lag, but to be honest, I would have been out running even if I hadn't been jet-lagged. I wouldn't have been able to help myself. I love to run. I love the endorphins. I love the way it clears my mind and all the stress just leaves my body. I love that I can do it anywhere my feet and my calling take me . . . in Greece on the shores of the Mediterranean Sea, in Cape Town in full view of the Atlantic, or where I grew up on the beaches of Australia.

For more than three decades, I have laced up my running shoes and raced out the door. To detox. To cleanse. To absorb. To explore. To keep my feet on the ground, in every way. Physically. Mentally. Emotionally. Spiritually. It's something my soul and my body seem to need. Though it hasn't always been that way.

Looking back, I think my love for running must have started the year I turned seventeen. I remember, like most of Australia and much of the world back then, I watched TV coverage of Cliff Young running in the 1983 Westfield Sydney to Melbourne Ultramarathon—a distance run covering 543.7 miles. It was inconceivable to me that anyone could run that far, particularly someone like Cliff.

I'll never forget how, just five days before the ultramarathon started, Cliff showed up, out of the blue. At first no one even noticed him among all the race enthusiasts. Like hundreds of others, he appeared to be just another spectator in the crowd. But when he registered to run and then arrived the morning of the race wearing overalls and rubber galoshes over his work boots, he was hard to overlook. He definitely stood out among the elite runners who were some of the most fit and competitive athletes in the world. Especially since they were all wearing professional gear provided by the top sporting brands in the world.

No one took Cliff seriously. Not the media. Not the race officials. Certainly not the other runners. How could they? Cliff was a sixty-one-year-old potato farmer who had lived his life tending two thousand sheep on two thousand acres on foot in his rubber boots. For most of his life, his family had not had money for horses or cars. When he was asked if he could run the race, his answer was simple: "Yes, I can."

Because of that, an entire nation tuned in to see if he really could, including me. To see his latest progress on the nightly news became sheer entertainment. At first, people weren't sure whether to laugh at him or cheer him on, but no matter, no one could quit watching. Along with millions of others, I sat glued to the TV every night, utterly captivated.

On the first day, when the starting pistol fired and the runners took off, Cliff shuffled off the starting line . . . literally. The media mocked him because he had a style all his own where he barely picked up his feet. And to top it off, he was running without his false teeth. He said they rattled when he ran. Race officials were certain he would keel over, so they followed his progress closely, ever ready to rescue him from a medical emergency.

In the first two days, it became apparent he didn't even know the rules of the race. Runners were conditioned to run for eighteen hours, then sleep for six. Because Cliff was so far behind in the beginning, thanks to his shuffling style, and because he didn't know he was supposed to stop at the eighteen-hour mark to sleep, he kept running . . . and only slept a couple of hours over the next two days! While the other runners ran and rested according to the schedule, Cliff kept running and eventually gained a lead.

By the fifth day, it felt like the entire world had joined Australia in rooting for the potato farmer. It seemed that everyone had begun to take him a little more seriously. He was still toothless, but he was still in the race—and he wasn't stopping. He'd been given a new pair of sneakers, a style of shoes he'd never run in before. He was now wearing shorts and a zipped jacket. His every move was being filmed—when he stopped to rest and when he ate as he ran. When one reporter asked him how he motivated himself to run for more than five days continuously without sleep, he said that he just imagined chasing the sheep around for days as he had as a kid on the farm when he needed to outrun a storm.

Near the end of the last day, when the news turned to the ultramarathon, Cliff was still in the lead. Unbelievable. When the reporters ran alongside him and placed a microphone in front of him, he seemed as surprised at his progress as they did. No doubt, what had seemed impossible was most likely going to happen—and it did.

Cliff Young finished the race having run five days, fifteen hours, and four minutes—the equivalent of four marathons a day—shattering the previous record by more than two days. When they awarded him the prize money of $10,000, he said he'd had no idea there was a prize. Because he felt all the runners had worked just as hard as he had, he gave each of the other five finalists $2,000, and he walked away with no cash.

Cliff became a national hero, of sorts, and his unconventional participation actually changed the way runners participated. From 1983 on, runners slept only three hours a night rather than six, though today most modern ultramarathon competitors don't sleep at all. And many runners adopted his shuffling style. It became clear that shuffling your way through a race was more aerodynamic and energy efficient. It was dubbed the "Young Shuffle."[1]

After the race was over, and the countless talk show interviews ensued, Cliff was asked a question we all wanted to know: "How did you do it?"

His answer has never left me: "I just never stopped. I kept going."

WE'RE RUNNING A RACE

To this day, I find it inspiring that Cliff didn't win the ultramarathon because of time he spent with the greatest trainers in the world. He didn't win because he was decked out in the latest gear. He didn't win because he was keto, vegan, vegetarian, or an intermittent faster. He won because he just kept going. He pressed on. Something he was able to do because he had pressed on over and over in the past. He'd built up endurance by chasing sheep his whole life. In the rain. In the mud. In the cold. In the blistering heat. When he felt like it and when he didn't. When he ran the race, he did what he'd always done, until he crossed the finish line and won.

I understand that most of us will never run a distance race like Cliff did, pounding the pavement for hundreds of miles, but spiritually speaking, we are in a race that's even more momentous. We are running a spiritual ultramarathon that will span the distance of a lifetime—and how we run that race will make all the difference in how we cross the finish line, or even if we will reach it at all.

We are running a spiritual ultramarathon that will span the distance of a lifetime—and how we run that race will make all the difference in how we cross the finish line, or even if we will reach it at all.

I know this because in verse after verse, the Bible likens our journey on this earth to a race and what it will take to run our individual races. When Paul wrote to the Corinthians, he gave them instructions on how they were to run: "Do you not know that those who run in a race all run, but one receives the prize? Run in such a way that you may obtain it" (1 Cor. 9:24 NKJV).

Speaking about how he was running his own race, he said, "I do not run like someone running aimlessly" (1 Cor. 9:26 NIV).

On another occasion he said, "However, I consider my life worth nothing to me; my only aim is to finish the race and complete the task the Lord Jesus has given me—the task of testifying to the good news of God's grace" (Acts 20:24 NIV).

When he had finished his race, at the end of his life, he wrote to his apprentice, Timothy, and said, "I have finished the race, I have kept the faith" (2 Tim. 4:7).

Encouraging the early Christians as well, the writer of Hebrews said, "Let us run with endurance the race that is set before us" (Heb. 12:1 ESV).

While all these verses show us that our lives are a spiritual race, what's equally important for us to understand is *how* we need to run our race so that we fulfill all the purposes and plans God has for us—so that we can obtain the prize. I, for one, don't want to miss out on one thing God has planned for me. When I wanted to ring the bell, imagine if I'd gone through with it. *What* would I have missed? *Who* would I have missed? Sometimes, in the moment of our distress, we don't always see what all is on the other side of our decisions. There are people God has assigned to us, people waiting to encounter Jesus' mercy, grace, love, kindness, justice, and generosity. How important it is to stay in the race, trusting God that we'll flourish if we do, impacting even more people with the gospel.

I am convinced that we must live our lives with the same intentionality as the apostle Paul, so we don't miss a single race God has for us. Paul ran with purpose. He was laser focused and determined, so much so, at one point, he said,

> Not that I have already obtained all this, or have already arrived at my goal, but I *press on* to take hold of that for which Christ Jesus took hold of me. Brothers and sisters, I do not consider myself yet to have taken hold of it. But one thing I do: Forgetting what is behind and straining toward what is ahead, I *press on* toward the goal to win the prize for which God has called me heavenward in Christ Jesus (Phil. 3:12–14 NIV, emphasis mine).

If we're going to run our race in such a way that we obtain the prize, then we will have to press on through everything that is pressing on us and against us. We will have to press on from where we are to where God wants us to go. We will have to press on through our flesh, through our feelings, and through our pain. We will have to press on through our ambitions, our desires, and our expectations. We will even have to press on through our successes—after all, it's the triumphs that oftentimes cause us to fall into apathy or complacency, pride or arrogance. In certain areas of our lives, in certain seasons of our lives, we will have to press play, pause, or stop, because pressing is how we will keep going.

When Paul said that we're to press on, he'd been through far more than I can comprehend. His race was not easy. When he wrote to the Philippians, he had already endured being flogged five times with thirty-nine lashes, beaten with rods three times, pelted with stones, and shipwrecked three times, in addition to spending twenty-four hours in open water. (I feel sure he would have passed Navy SEAL training with that one!) He had experienced danger from bandits, fellow Jews, and Gentiles alike. He knew what it was to go without sleep, to hunger, and to thirst. He had endured being cold and naked (2 Cor. 11:23–27). And still, he wrote the most positive, faith-filled anthem: "I press on."

I personally have not had to undergo any of the things Paul did as I've run my race, nor do I ever want to. I'm sure you don't either, but we all have a race to run, and therefore, things we must continually press through. Each person's race is unique and distinct, full of highs and lows, pleasure and pain, joy and suffering, trials and tribulations, blessings and mystery. But as Cliff Young showed us, there is only one way to finish a race, and that is to never stop and to just keep going.

Cliff made it look so easy, especially from my vantage point, sitting on the couch watching TV. His shuffling along made it look so effortless, so natural, but it rarely looks that way for us. I think we sometimes romanticize this spiritual race and think there will be no bumps on the road, no potholes, hurdles, obstacles, or detours, but there often are.

This race can seem overwhelming and daunting at times, I know. I wish I could tell you it will be easy, or that it will get easier as we go, but I can't. Perhaps exhilarating or adventurous? Yes. But easy? No. I wish I could recommend some powerful supplement from the root of the running plant, but I have yet to find it. I wish there was another way—any other way—to win our race other than pressing on, because we all know we'd much rather be carried.

I've said that I love to run, and at the beginning of this chapter, I painted a beautiful picture of how invigorating it is, but to be even more honest, by the time I finish a really good run, I'm about to pass out. If someone would offer to carry me back to the house or the hotel or wherever I'm staying, I would be all-in. But Paul put it out there for us. He said it not once but twice, so we would really get it.

"I *press on* to take hold of that for which Christ Jesus took hold of me."

"I *press on* toward the goal to win the prize."

Never one to miss an opportunity to insert a Greek word, the root meaning for *press* in this text is *dioko*, which means "to pursue, to chase, to hunt down."[2] Therefore, when Paul pressed on, he pursued, chased, and hunted down the One who had captured his heart. He pressed on to win the prize, which is Jesus. In the same way, if we're going to run our race to win the prize, if we're going to cross the finish line, then we will need to pursue more of Jesus with all our hearts. None of us can run our race in our own strength. We need more of him in order to keep running after him. But get this: Jesus never meant for us to run our race alone, and he promised that he would be with us always—to the very end of the age (Matt. 28:20). So as we're running hard after him, he's in fact with us every step of the way. It really doesn't get any better than that.

Since Jesus is the anchor of our souls, pressing on toward him is one more way we stay tethered to him and his purpose for our lives. It's one more way we stop ourselves from drifting because, like I mentioned in chapter 1, all we have to do to start drifting is nothing. Just as ocean currents can carry us to places we never intended to go, if we don't press on for more of Jesus, then the currents of our time will take us wherever they are headed. We will inadvertently start *coasting*, which, by definition, means we will be "moving forward using no power."[3]

Jesus never meant for us to live on this earth powerless. He knew we would need help, and he provided it. When Jesus left this earth, he gave us the Holy Spirit—the same Spirit who raised him from the dead—to live in us and help us run our race (John 16:7; Rom. 8:11; 1 Cor. 3:16). To give us power—power to overcome the Enemy, to resist temptation, to defeat fear, and to do the things God has called us to do (Luke 9:12; Acts 1:8; 2 Tim. 1:7). We literally have his resurrection power living inside of us! Think of how we need his strength, his might, his power to overcome and keep moving forward in every area of our lives. Every single day. Why would any of us ever want to move along without using all the power God has made available to us?

Since we are in the final chapter of this book, and by now you know that I do not want anyone to drift away from Jesus or his purpose, I want you to take a moment and ask yourself if perhaps you have ceased pressing on in some area of your life. Are you simply coasting along, going through the motions, but no longer feeling passionate in your pursuit of Jesus and all he has for your life? Can you identify an area in your life where you have stopped taking risks and stepping out in faith? An area where, perhaps, instead of pressing on, you've pulled back? An area where the pain, cost, loss, or disappointment far outweigh the pleasure of the pursuit? It's so easy to turn on the autopilot and let the current of society, our feelings, or our desires take us wherever they are going. Especially when we're hurting.

We all go through things that can cause us to do this, to drift. Through the pages of this book, I've done my best to demonstrate how easily it can happen. At the same time, I would be remiss if I didn't mention that we also can stop pressing on when we aren't suffering and times are good. It's only natural. Without something pressing in on us, it's easy to find ourselves coasting, being pushed along with the currents, letting them take us wherever they are going. When everything is going well, it's easy to start doing nothing, but our nothing is always something, isn't it?

What do we do when there's no pain in our hearts or pressure bearing down on us? When there's no emergency, no crisis, no challenge? When there's money in the bank, food on the table, and a vacation on the horizon? When we've climbed the corporate ladder and our careers are on the upswing? When we've started the business we always planned? When our marriages are happy, and our kids are well? Or when we're enjoying the single life, perhaps even traveling to all the places we've dreamed of? Taking the college courses we always wanted to take, in the university we always hoped to attend? The point is, we can start to drift just as easily when everything is going great, when we're in a season that is exactly what we prayed for and quite possibly what we worked so hard for.

Maybe it's time for us to check our markers, you know, like my dad taught us kids to do at Umina Beach. To look up and see where we are and how far we might have drifted.

If you suspect you have pulled back—regardless of the reason or the circumstances—you have to know that however far from Jesus you may feel you have drifted, it is never too far. He sees. He knows. He cares. You're still within his reach, and he wants to help you drop and set anchor. This book is in your hands at this moment in time, in the place where you are, for a reason. My prayer for you is that God will breathe on these words to open your broken, shattered, or hardened heart to the delight of chasing down his Son again.

IT'S TIME TO PRESS

There is no doubt that when I came to that moment where I seriously contemplated ringing the bell, what I was saying was that I was tired of pressing on. I momentarily wondered if the pressing on was worth it. I had been pressing on for decades, and I had been feeling the pressure of it in a heightened way for a couple of years straight. I just didn't think I could take it anymore. As I mentioned at the beginning of this book, I wasn't having a crisis of faith; I didn't want to walk away from Jesus or even our ministry. I wasn't going to massively backslide. I just wanted to stop pressing and, therefore, invariably, simply coast to the finish line. No more risk-taking. No more pioneering. No more believing God to do the impossible. No more real sacrificial living. I imagined that overseeing our work from a dreamy little café in Greece, situated perfectly on the island of Santorini, would be preferable to the energy required to press on.

I knew that if I kept going the way I had always gone, all-in, holding nothing back, it would invariably mean more pain, more heartache, more exposure, more vulnerability, more attacks.

I didn't know if I wanted to keep pressing through any more weariness, disappointment, disillusionment, offense, hurt, failure, mistakes, rejection, loss, grief, betrayal, or the unknown, unplanned, uncharted territory that was certain to be ahead. I would have preferred to settle into things that were safe and secure, to find contentment in the predictable and doable, to start coasting, no longer pressing on. And, besides, I really love watching the sunset in Santorini.

I was shocked by my own response. I had never thought I would reach a place where I would even contemplate not pressing on. But, momentarily, I lost sight of Jesus, mostly because my heart was broken and I felt vulnerable, confused, weary, and weak. When you lose sight of the One you are running for and with and toward, pressing on no longer seems to be worth the pain. Wouldn't you agree that the only reason any of us would crucify our flesh, deny ourselves, be obedient, remain faithful, and keep pressing on is because of Jesus? If it were not for him, then, seriously, none of this would be worth it. Not at all. It is too big a price to pay for anyone or anything else. It's only when we look up and fix our eyes on Jesus, and Jesus alone, that we can see how pressing on is so worthwhile. For me, that's how I found the strength and courage not to ring the bell.

Still, when I decided to press on, I knew it would be painful. But I also knew that greater pressing would produce greater fruitfulness—and deep down, I wanted to bring God greater glory by producing more fruit. I knew that since I was still alive and breathing, God must have more fruit for me to produce. After

> It's only when we look up and fix our eyes on Jesus, and Jesus alone, that we can see how pressing on is so worthwhile.

all, Jesus told us, it is to our Father's glory that we bear *much* fruit (John 15:8). And since there doesn't appear to be an expiration date on this in Scripture, as long as we're alive, there will always be more fruit to bear. Once we press on through one thing, we might get a reprieve, but the reward for passing the pressing test is more pressing—and more fruit.

It helps me to picture it this way: Grapes are crushed to make wine. Diamonds are formed under pressure. And best of all, the staple food of Greek culture—olives—are pressed into olive oil.

When I was growing up, olive oil was an essential ingredient in Mum's kitchen, and to this day, I enjoy a strong and flavorful olive oil on salads, tomatoes, cheese, almost anything. I even love the smell of fresh olives. One of my favorite times to be in the southern region of Europe is when the sweet olive trees smell the strongest—right before the olives are harvested. The air all around them is pungent, and it's one of my favorite scents. I suppose even my sense of smell knows I'm Greek.

But to get flavorful, robust extra virgin olive oil (EVOO), olives have to be pressed. They have to be crushed. They have to endure being transformed from one state to another. Not to get too detailed, but to give you an idea of what I mean, initially, after olives are harvested from the trees, they are quickly cleaned and pressed into a paste, pits and all—either with an ancient method of a grinding wheel weighing hundreds of pounds or with modern industrial equipment. The paste is then spread onto fibrous cloths that are layered one on top of the other, where they are pressed even more with pounds and pounds of pressure so intense that every drop of oil is squeezed out.

But even after all that, the oil goes through another kind of pressing. It's heated—just high enough but not too high—so the impurities fall to the bottom and the EVOO rises to the top. It's silky, beautifully colored, and ready to be stored where it can rest. Much like the taste-testing of a fine wine, the olive oil is tasted to ensure its quality.[4] Later, when it has rested long enough, it is bottled into green or dark-colored glass—the perfect color to block harmful UV rays that can spoil it.

The best-tasting olive oil is made when the olives are picked at just the right time, crushed quickly into a paste, pressed again at just the right intervals, heated to just the right temperature, cooled for just the right amount of time, and then bottled at the right moment. No doubt, to make the perfect bottle of oil requires the right amount of pressing at all the right times.

In similar fashion, for us to run our race in such a way that we obtain the prize, we're going to have to be pressed with the right amount of pressing at all the right times—and then, what really will determine how much of the prize we obtain is how we respond to the pressing. If we want to grow, if we want to become more like Christ, if we want him to fill more of us with more of him, if we want to fulfill all the plans and purposes of God for our lives, then we will choose to endure the pressing and press on . . .

- Past our past.
- Past our fleshly tendencies.
- Past our fears.
- Past our mistakes.
- Past our failures.
- Past our disappointments.
- Past our hurts.
- Past our insecurities.
- Past the pain.

- Past our successes.
- Past our comfort zones.
- Past our complacency.
- Past our familiarity.
- Past whatever is holding us back.

Past whatever is pressing against us. Looking to Jesus. Reaching for more of Jesus. Running hard after him. It's so easy for us to think, *If I just press on this one time, or press through this one thing, then I'll be home free*, but while we are still breathing, there is still more pressing.

Looking back, in every single season and stage of my Christian life and ministry, God has always required me to press on through things when I would have preferred to be delivered out of them. But it was the pressing process that produced the necessary anointing and character formation required for me to do the next thing God called me to do. All through the pressing process, God has continuously prepared me for the things he had prepared for me. He's been so faithful to get me ready for the next leg of my race.

WE HAVE NEED OF ENDURANCE

I love to land in a new city, lace up my running shoes, and hit the pavement, though many times it has led to unexpected adventures. You would think that I'd learn, but on more than one occasion, I've gotten lost and had to run much farther than I ever thought I could to find my way back to where I started. It's been in those moments, when I've exhausted myself to the point where I didn't think I could take another step, that I've imagined myself a marathon runner who has hit a wall and has to power on through the miles. At times, I've even imagined myself breaking the tape. It's a grand illusion, I know, as I'm not *that* serious of a runner. Still, I have known what it's like to think I'm going to collapse. That I can't possibly go on. That I can't keep going. And yet, each time, I have found the strength. I've never been so lost I couldn't get back.

I have found the same to be true as I have run my spiritual race. So many times, I have hit a wall and thought, *I'm done. I can't go on. I can't go one more step.* And yet, somehow, someway, I did, though it was never in my own strength. It was always in his strength, but his strength that's been built on the inside of me.

In other words, all the years of pressing on have produced a strength in my life that can't be produced any other way. It has produced *endurance*, something Paul said we would have need of to run our race (Heb. 10:36). Something that keeps us going, even when we don't think we can keep going. Looking back, I feel sure this was a big part of why I didn't ring the bell. Though I didn't fully understand how I'd gotten to where I had ended up, I had pressed on for so many years that I couldn't help but keep pressing on. Endurance kicked in and kept me moving forward. It's what helped me push through each and every wall that I couldn't see past.

It works the same in all our lives. When we press through over and over, pressing on for more of Jesus, we grow stronger spiritually. We build endurance, a critical component to our race. *Endurance* is "the ability to withstand hardship or adversity."[5] It's the capacity and power to bear up under difficult circumstances. It's a hopeful fortitude that perseveres to the end. In the original

Greek language of the New Testament, it is *hupomone*, a compound word that translates "to remain under."[6] It is a quality built by remaining under pressure, something our natural inclination wants to drift away from. Don't we all prefer comfort and ease? Don't we all want to escape when the pressure becomes too great? I know I do, but with life comes pressure. I did not build spiritual strength by doing the things that came easy to me, but by overcoming the things I did not think I could. It's how I grew in faith. I feel sure it's how you've grown in your faith too.

Sometimes we just need to remember how far we've come to run the next leg of our race. That's basically what the writer of Hebrews said: "But recall the former days when, after you were enlightened, *you endured a hard struggle*. . . . Therefore do not throw away your confidence, which has a great reward. *For you have need of endurance*" (Heb. 10:32, 35–36 ESV, emphasis added). There's only one way to build endurance, and that's by pressing on—again and again.

> I did not build spiritual strength by doing the things that came easy to me, but by overcoming the things I did not think I could.

Imagine how nice it would be if endurance were an app. Wouldn't it be great if we could just tap it open and request it like we do everything else we need? If we want a ride, there's an app. If we want to make reservations at a restaurant, there's an app. If we want groceries, a TV show or movie, news, sports, or weather, there's an app. But for endurance, there is no app. I've checked! It's not something that can be downloaded. It's a strength that can only be built when we stay with something when all we really want to do is quit. It is a strength that is built only through resistance. Believe me, every time my trainer adds more weight to the bar, I groan. But my muscles will grow stronger only if I press against more resistance.

Except for a rare few in this world, life generally does not go as planned. It's full of curveballs, unexpected challenges, loss, disappointment, grief, and turmoil. If you've read any of my other books, then you know that my life has been anything but trouble-free and pain-free. I would love to say there is always an easy path forward, but experience and Scripture tell us that is not how it usually is. We live in a fallen world, and trials are part of living in this world. Therefore, we will have troubles; we will make mistakes; we will experience disappointments; we will have loss; we will grow weary; we will want to ring the bell; we will want to quit. We will find ourselves in a place asking, *How did I get here?* But if we keep pressing on and building endurance, then we will have the strength to not drop out of our race. We will have the strength to not quit.

I know that Jesus came to this earth fully divine and yet fully man (Col. 2:9; Heb. 1:3). The theological term for this profound mystery is *hypostatic union*. Though Jesus walked this earth as our Savior, he also walked it fully human, capable of being intimately acquainted with the frailties of our humanity. In other words, he knew then and he knows now what it is to feel what we feel. The writer of Hebrews described him this way: "For we do not have a high priest who is unable to sympathize with our weaknesses, but one who has been tempted in every way as we are, yet without sin" (4:15). When Jesus was on earth, he felt it all: grief (John 11:35), temptation (Mark 1:13), frustration (John 2:15–16), weariness (Luke 13:34), rejection (John 6:66), sorrow (Matt. 26:38), ridicule (Mark 15:19), loneliness (Matt. 27:46). And yet, he endured. Just as he calls us to do all throughout our lives.

- When he first started out, he was tempted by the Devil for forty days in the wilderness, and yet he endured (Mark 1:13).
- When his own family did not understand what he was doing and thought he was crazy, he endured (John 7:5).
- When his followers began to fall away one by one, he endured (John 6:66).
- When he was dishonored in his own hometown, he endured (Mark 6:1–6).
- When the Pharisees lied about him and the Sadducees conspired to trap him, he endured (Luke 20; John 8).
- When Judas, one of his twelve closest friends, betrayed him, he endured (Matt. 26:14–15; 27:3–5).
- When he faced a trial and was sentenced, he endured (Matt. 26:47–68; 27:11–26).
- When he was tortured, he endured (Mark 15:16–32).

And he never quit. Even when he was crucified, he endured. He crossed his finish line. He fulfilled his assignment. He died, was buried, and rose from the dead, fulfilling prophecy about the Messiah (1 Cor. 15:4). He then took his seat in heaven at the right hand of the Father (Heb. 10:12).

If Jesus could endure his entire race, then I know that we can, too, and not just because he became fully man and demonstrated it for us—but because we are filled with the Holy Spirit! We are filled with the power to press on!

Paul said for us to run our race in such a way that we win the prize, and the only way to do that is to simply keep going. Keep pressing on. Keep enduring. Keep running hard after Jesus—anchoring ourselves in him deeper and deeper—until we cross our finish line. Jesus alone is the reason we keep pressing on, running our race. Jesus alone is worthy of our endurance. He alone is worthy of our devotion, our faithfulness, our praise, and our pressing on to obtain more of him. To this day, the angels go round his throne declaring his majesty: "Holy, holy, holy, Lord God, the Almighty, who was, who is, and who is to come" (Rev. 4:8). They cast their crowns before his throne saying, "Our Lord and God, you are worthy to receive glory and honor and power, because you have created all things, and by your will they exist and were created" (Rev. 4:11).

What a day it will be when we cross our finish line and get to cast our crowns before his feet too (James 1:12; 1 Peter 5:4; Rev. 3:11). For that, we cannot stop running our race. For that we cannot stop pressing on. For that we cannot stop enduring. Jesus is the One who is worthy of our all. He is the prize!

CONCLUSION

Let's Ring the Bells of Victory!

For bells are the voice of the church;
They have tones that touch and search
The hearts of young and old.

—HENRY WADSWORTH LONGFELLOW, "THE BELLS OF SAN BLAS"

Closing my eyes, lifting my head slightly to let my face bask in the sun, I attempted to immortalize the magnificent panorama before me. I wanted this moment and the view to live on forever, like a photo I could store on my phone and pull out anytime I needed a minivacation. There was nowhere on earth more picture-perfect to me. The still, azure Aegean waters. The stunning clusters of white stucco clinging to the cliffs. The scattered domes mirroring the perfect blue. The glowing sunset resting on it all. You guessed it. I was in my favorite place in all the world. *Santorini.*

Standing atop one of the highest points along the caldera, a thousand feet above sea level, Nick and I had been hiking the trail from Oia to Fira when I was compelled to stop and soak in the breathtaking vista. We'd been coming here for years, ever since our honeymoon, every chance we had to pass through this part of the world. Not once did it disappoint.

Just as I was about to open my eyes for one final sweep, I couldn't help but catch my breath when I heard the most majestic sound. One I have loved since childhood. To me, it was a holy beckoning and the perfect touch to our beautiful morning. The church bells were ringing. Not just at one church but at every church. I could hear the ones up close and the ones in the distance. All across the island in all the villages. As though one was calling to the other. Shouting the noon hour as loudly as they could. In the midst of the ringing, I could hear the melodious peal from the Three Bells of Fira just below us in the village of Firostefani. The three separate bells stack high into a tower of arches, hovering on a cliff overlooking the sea. Though I had no idea how long they had stood there, the church was built in the 1700s, and together, the bells had served centuries of worshippers. Looking down at them, I couldn't help but linger a bit longer and give them all the reverence they deserved.

Growing up hearing the bells rung high atop our Greek Orthodox church, I suppose I was destined to love the noble sounds of church bells—whether the gongs from a single bell or from a perfectly timed carillon. No matter where I've heard them, they've always brought me a sense of peace. It's as though they stir hope in me. No doubt, they act as a reminder that God is at work in the world, and that there are people everywhere seeking him, serving him, and answering his call to come.

THE CALL TO COME

For centuries, church bells have had deeply symbolic meaning, and though there are no church bells mentioned in the Bible, we know from the Old Testament that small gold bells were strung along the bottom of the high priest's garment, interspersed with pomegranates, so that he could be heard moving around in the holy of holies—the place inside the temple where only the high priest could go (Ex. 28:33–35).

We also know there is coming a day when Jesus will return and establish the kingdom of God on earth. When he does, as the prophet Zechariah foretold, those who gather to God will find themselves at peace with his creation, and even more bells will ring—ones that declare his holiness.[1] "And on that day there shall be inscribed on the bells of the horses, 'Holy to the LORD.' And the pots in the house of the LORD shall be as the bowls before the altar" (Zech. 14:20 ESV).

I think it's marvelous that church bells have been woven into our history. They have been rung throughout the world, calling people to pray. Calling them to remember. Calling them to come. Since the Middle Ages, they have been rung to celebrate births, weddings, and holy days. Isn't it just beautiful when a couple exits the church for the first time as husband and wife and the bells toll? To me, it may very well be the best part of the ceremony.

Church bells have been used to mark the beginning, middle, and end of a day—especially before it was common for people to own timepieces or wear wristwatches. In some churches, bells have been rung three times a day—morning, noon, and night—to call people to pray the Lord's Prayer.[2] They have been used to mourn the lost or call people to town meetings.[3] They have been used to call children to school or to come in from recess. They have announced to entire villages the time to plant and the time to harvest. Though they were silenced during World War II, Great Britain rang her church bells to warn of an aerial attack, and at the end of the war, all the bells throughout Europe rang continuously and gloriously, celebrating the Allied victory.

To this day, we still ring all kinds of bells for a myriad of reasons. To start sporting events or to celebrate the wins. To cheer on our teams and make all the noise we can. There's nothing quite like a pep rally full of cowbells to shout school spirit. I'll never forget how bells were rung during the 2020 coronavirus pandemic to thank health-care workers serving on the front lines.[4] It was a moving tribute in a time when we couldn't meet with any of them physically and thank them ourselves.

When we enter a store, we sometimes hear the little shopkeeper's bell tinkle overhead, and when we need customer service, we know to tap the bell sitting on the counter. Even at the New York Stock Exchange, a bell is rung to start and stop each trading day.

One of the most moving traditions to me is when a cancer patient rings the bell at a treatment center to celebrate being declared cancer-free. It's a tradition begun by a rear admiral in the United States Navy, Irve Le Moyne. In 1996, he told his doctor that he planned to follow a navy tradition of ringing a bell to signify "when the job was done." So, at his last treatment, he brought a brass bell and rang it several times, then left it as a donation. It was later mounted on a wall with this inscription:

Ring this bell
Three times well
Its toll to clearly say,

CONCLUSION

My treatment's done
This course is run
And I am on my way!⁵

Maybe you've known the privilege of ringing such a bell, or perhaps you celebrated with a friend or family member. What a feeling it must have been "when the job was done"!

In the work of A21, every time a man, woman, or child is rescued from human trafficking, our team rings a bell. In every office around the world. We cheer, clap, hoot, and holler. We celebrate the victory as loudly as we can. It's our way of taking five and giving thanks. Our team members are so committed, and they work so hard, it's only fitting to acknowledge when their efforts save a life. Not long ago, after a hundred of our team members and interns at our California commercial office building were shouting and cheering about a rescue, one of our team members was stopped downstairs by someone who works in the office under ours. He wanted to know why we make so much noise from time to time. It was a fair question. After our team member explained, the office downstairs made it their practice to join in—they do it every time they hear us ring the bell. I can't tell you how this thrills us all. We believe we are to be salt and light and to make a difference in this world, and now the office downstairs is celebrating with us. What a gift!

The ringing of bells in my life has come to mean more than ever. I'm grateful that when I drifted, when I felt so unsure of whether I could keep going the way I had always gone, when I wanted to ring the bell of defeat, God did not allow me to do it. Instead, in his great mercy, he helped me anchor my soul even deeper in him so I could continue to ring the bells of victory everywhere God calls me to go.

I want to ring the bells of salvation and freedom. I want to ring the bells of faith, hope, and love. I want to ring the bells of goodness, kindness, and gentleness. I want to ring the bells of patience, faithfulness, and trust. I want to ring the bells of mercy and forgiveness, of healing and deliverance. I want to ring the bells of grace, reconciliation, and restoration. I want to ring the bells of truth and justice. I want to keep ringing each and every bell of the gospel, because . . .

- Jesus is alive.
- Jesus saves.
- Jesus heals.
- Jesus redeems.
- Jesus restores.
- Jesus reconciles.
- Jesus is good.
- Jesus does good.
- Jesus is holy.
- Jesus is just.
- Jesus is merciful.
- Jesus is worthy.

Until Jesus comes again, he wants us to keep ringing the bells of victory! At my age, in the second half of my life, I know that ringing all the bells God has called me to ring will require more risk. It will require more faith. But I'm up for it, and I'm going after it. We weren't created to live safe, boring, comfortable, or predictable lives. We were created and transformed to be risk-takers—people who live by faith, walk by faith, and go out into our world to share our faith. So I'm staying on mission, advancing the mission of God on the earth. I want to fulfill all the purpose, plans, and good works God has for me. I want to help bring in a harvest of souls. I want my daughters—both natural and spiritual—to see that Jesus is worthy of it all. I want to do justice everywhere I see injustice. I want to bring God all the glory that I can.

Will it be hard?

Yes.

Will it be painful?

Yes.

Will it be worth it?

Always.

I know that I am not alone. And neither are you. The hour is urgent, and I'm ready. After all I've been through, after the ways I've drifted and been tempted to drift, I know I am now anchored in Christ more than ever. I am certain of the strength of the Anchor to keep me—and you—in this rapidly shifting world, in spite of the currents, winds, and waves. Jesus has proved himself faithful, strong, dependable, and trustworthy, over and over again. Jesus is the One holding me, and he is the One who will keep me from ever quitting. I stand ready to ring every bell that brings God glory and celebrates his victory.

> I know that ringing all the bells God has called me to ring will require more risk. It will require more faith. But I'm up for it.

ACKNOWLEDGMENTS

It takes a team to help an author birth a vision. I am so grateful to God for everyone who had a hand in this project from start to finish.

To my husband, Nick: Thank you for helping me keep going and not ring the bell. Only you and Jesus know how close I really came. No one has believed in me, encouraged me, carried me, or pushed me more than you. After a quarter of a century together, I feel like we are just getting started.

To my girls, Catherine and Sophia: I am so grateful God picked me to be your mum. You are the absolute delight of my life. Thank you for your support and patience once again through the writing process. This time was harder because we were all in quarantine together and the kitchen island was my writing desk, which impacted how many times you could open the fridge in a day. You made it fun when it should have been stressful and even let me tell some of your stories. I love you both with all my heart.

To Elizabeth Prestwood: No one knows everything I have taught and said more than you do. You push me to dig deep and help me to better express my thoughts and words. Having you alongside me as a collaborative writer, helping me carry the project and bring the stories to life, makes all the difference. Because of you, this book is better.

To Lysa TerKeurst: I could never thank you enough for taking our team through your COMPEL Training experience. This book would not be what it is had you not helped us. I love you dearly, my friend. Thank you for spurring me on to be and do better.

To Rebekah Layton: Thank you for reviewing every chapter numerous times. You offered so much wisdom and made great suggestions. You mean the world to me, and I deeply appreciate your commitment to this message.

To Rosilyn, Katie, Emily, Jess, Natalie, Mi Yung, Noah, Andrea, and Rhiannon: Thank you for generously sharing your stories and letting your experiences inspire us all.

To Tim Paulson, Jamie Lockard, Jessica Wong, Brigitta Nortker, Whitney Bak, Stephanie Tresner, Kristen Golden, Claire Drake, Sara Broun, and the whole team at Thomas Nelson: Thank you for welcoming me into the family with open arms. You poured your heart and soul into this project with great passion and enthusiasm. Jessica, you are the world's best editor, and your suggestions helped to strengthen this work. I am so grateful for each and every one of you.

To Matt Yates: Thank you for believing in this message and helping me dream bigger and reach further. You have been a huge gift to Nick and me. We are so grateful you are in our world.

To our A21, Propel, ZOE Church, and Equip and Empower teams, volunteers, partners, and supporters: Serving Jesus alongside you is the greatest privilege and honor of my life. A special thank-you to Ashley Ziegler and Katie Strandlund, who worked tirelessly to ensure all the pieces of the puzzle came together. I love y'all so very much.

To my Lord and Savior, Jesus Christ: You are this hope I have, as an anchor for my soul.

NOTES

INTRODUCTION

1. Keith Scott-Mumby, "Two Thirds of People Who Drown Are Strong Swimmers," Dr. Keith Scott-Mumby: The Alternative Doctor, https://alternative-doctor.com/news-stuff/two-thirds-of-people-who-drown-are-strong-swimmers/.

CHAPTER 1: DROPPING—AND SETTING—ANCHOR

1. "Ocean Currents," National Oceanic and Atmospheric Administration, August 2011, https://www.noaa.gov/education/resource-collections/ocean-coasts/ocean-currents.
2. *Encyclopaedia Britannica Online*, s.v. "East Australian Current," February 21, 2019, https://www.britannica.com/place/East-Australian-Current; "East Australian Current," Earth Observatory, August 17, 2005, https://earthobservatory.nasa.gov/images/15366/east-australian-current.
3. "Chains: General Information," Anchor Marine Houston, https://anchormarinehouston.com/wp-content/uploads/2019/03/Section_2_Chains.pdf; Katy Stickland, "How Much Anchor Chain?," *Yachting Monthly*, August 26, 2019, https://www.yachtingmonthly.com/sailing-skills/how-much-anchor-chain-70603; Fortress Marine Anchors, Guardian Anchors Selection Guide, https://fortressanchors.com/anchors/guardian/#guardianselection.

CHAPTER 2: YOU STOP TRUSTING AND YOU START CONTROLLING

1. David Fiedler, "What Is a Bike Chain Master Link and What Does It Do?," LiveAbout, updated February 8, 2019, https://www.liveabout.com/what-is-a-bike-chain-master-link-and-what-does-it-do-365498.

2. *King James Bible Dictionary*, s.v. "trust," http://www.kingjames bibledictionary.com/Dictionary/trust.

3. N. T. Wright, *Surprised by Hope: Rethinking Heaven, the Resurrection, and the Mission of the Church* (New York: HarperOne, 2008), 132–37.

4. Sean Grover, "Do You Have a Controlling Personality?," *Psychology Today*, November 30, 2017, https://www.psychologytoday.com/us/blog/when-kids-call-the-shots/201711/do-you-have-controlling-personality.

5. Grover.

6. Jack Wellman, "What Does Lament Mean? A Biblical Definition of Lament or Lamenting," Patheos, August 20, 2015, https://www.patheos.com/blogs/christiancrier/2015/08/20/what-does-lament-mean-a-biblical-definition-of-lament-or-lamenting/.

7. "Why Did Jesus Cry?" Bible Study, https://www.biblestudy.org/basicart/why-did-jesus-cry.html.

8. *King James Bible Dictionary*, s.v. "Lament," http://www.kingjames bibledictionary.com/Dictionary/lament.

9. *King James Bible Dictionary*.

10. Mark Vroegop, "Dare to Hope in God," Desiring God, April 6, 2019, https://www.desiringgod.org/articles/dare-to-hope-in-god.

11. N. T. Wright, "Christianity Offers No Answers About the Coronavirus. It's Not Supposed To," *TIME*, March 29, 2020, https://time.com/5808495/coronavirus-christianity/.

12. Mark Vroegop, "Lament Psalms Are a Gift," Mark Vroegop (website), http://markvroegop.com/lament-psalms-are-a-gift/; Ernie Baker, "Psalms 42 and 43—The Gift of Lament," Biblical Counseling Coalition, April 3, 2019, https://www.biblical counselingcoalition.org/2019/04/03/psalms-42-and-43-the-gift-of-lament/; Dr. Heath Thomas, "Lamentations and the Gift of

Prayer," Bible Society, November 18, 2016, https://www.bible
society.org.uk/explore-the-bible/bible-articles/lamentations-and
-the-gift-of-prayer/.

13. Wright, *Surprised by Hope*, 29.

14. Christine Caine, *20/20: Seen. Chosen. Sent.* (Nashville: Lifeway,
2019), 173.

CHAPTER 3: YOU STOP HEALING AND YOU START SEEPING

1. "About the Race," Absa Cape Epic, https://www.cape-epic.com
/riders/new-riders/about-the-race.

2. Christine Caine, 20/20: Seen. Chosen. Sent. (Nashville: Lifeway,
2019), 89.

3. J. Josh Smith, "Seeing Jesus Clearly: A Sermon from Mark 8:22–33,"
Southwestern Journal of Theology 53 (Spring 2011), https://preaching
source.com/journal/seeing-jesus-clearly-a-sermon-from-mark
-8-22-33/.

4. Smith.

CHAPTER 4: YOU STOP WONDERING AND YOU START WANDERING

1. "What Are the Most Famous/Important Questions in the Bible?"
Got Questions, https://www.gotquestions.org/questions-in-the
-Bible.html; Doug Andre, "The Most Important Question in the
Bible," Unlocking the Bible, January 6, 2016, https://unlocking
thebible.org/2016/01/the-most-important-question-in-the-bible/.

CHAPTER 5: YOU STOP PRAYING AND YOU START TALKING

1. "LSD," Drugs.com, https://www.drugs.com/illicit/lsd.html.

2. John Knox, *The Works of John Knox*, vol. 3, *Earliest Writings 1548–
1554*, ed. David Laing (Edinburgh: Bannatyne Club, 1854), 83.

3. "What Was the Temple Veil? What Is the Meaning of the Temple
Veil Being Torn in Two When Jesus Died?," CompellingTruth.
org, https://www.compellingtruth.org/temple-veil-torn.html.

4. *Encyclopaedia Britannica Online*, s.v. "Herod Agrippa I," January 1,
2021, https://www.britannica.com/biography/Herod-Agrippa-I.

CHAPTER 6: YOU STOP GATHERING AND YOU START ISOLATING

1. Brian Candy, "Christianity—Attending Church in Qatar," Qatar Quick, July 1, 2019, https://qatarquick.com/christianity-attending-church-in-qatar.

2. Caryle Murphy, "For the First Time, Christians in Qatar Worship in Church," *Christian Science Monitor*, February 9, 2009, https://www.csmonitor.com/World/Middle-East/2009/0209/p01s01-wome.html.

3. Caryle Murphy, "Qatar Opens First Church, Quietly," Al Jazeera, June 20, 2008, https://www.aljazeera.com/news/2008/06/20/qatar-opens-first-church-quietly/.

4. Oishimaya Sen Nag, "What Religions Are Practiced in Qatar?," World Atlas, April 23, 2018, https://www.worldatlas.com/articles/what-religions-are-practiced-in-qatar.html.

5. Dr. Steven Um et al., "The Background and Purpose of Hebrews," Thirdmill, https://thirdmill.org/seminary/lesson.asp?vs=HEB&ln=1.

6. Matt Merker, "Why Gather? Thinking About Gathering When Churches Can't," 9Marks, April 24, 2020, https://www.9marks.org/article/why-gather-thinking-about-gathering-when-churches-cant/.

7. W. E. Vine, *Vine's Expository Dictionary of Old and New Testament Words* (Grand Rapids: Revell, 1981), s.v. "ekklesia."

8. Merker, "Why Gather?"

9. Jonathan Leeman, "The Church Gathered," The Gospel Coalition, https://www.thegospelcoalition.org/essay/the-church-gathered/.

10. Merker, "Why Gather?"

11. Everett Ferguson, *The Church of Christ: A Biblical Ecclesiology for Today* (Grand Rapids: Eerdmans, 1996), 235.

12. Merker, "Why Gather?"

13. Fritz Chery, "12 Biblical Reasons for Attending Church," Bible Reasons, October 15, 2020, https://biblereasons.com/reasons-for-attending-church/.

14. Leeman, "The Church Gathered."

15. Leeman.

16. Ryan Holeywell, "In Houston, the Land of Megachurches, Religious Service Attendance Declines," Kinder Institute for

Urban Research, April 25, 2016, https://kinder.rice.edu/2016/04/25/in-houston-the-land-of-megachurches-fewer-people-attending-religious-services.

17. Dan Reiland, "5 Reasons People Drift from Church and How to Respond," *Outreach Magazine*, June 20, 2019, https://outreachmagazine.com/features/leadership/43753-5-reasons-people-drift-from-church-and-how-to-respond.html.

CHAPTER 7: YOU STOP HUNGERING AND YOU START GORGING

1. Omaira Gill, "Breaking Bread in Greece," Greece Is, March 16, 2016, https://www.greece-is.com/breaking-bread-greece/.

2. Nancy Gaifyllia, "Prosforo Orthodox Offering Bread," The Spruce Eats, August 13, 2019, https://www.thespruceeats.com/orthodox-offering-bread-1705604; Andrew Athanasiou, "Role of Bread in the Orthodox Church," Greek Boston, https://www.greekboston.com/religion/prosforo/; John Lardas, "Prosphora Bread Ministry," Holy Trinity Orthodox Church, https://orthodoxct.org/prosphora_bread.

3. Merrill, R. (2014). *Seeking.* Douglas Mangum, Derek R. Brown, Rachel Klippenstein, and Rebekah Hurst, eds., *Lexham Theological Wordbook* (Bellingham, WA: Lexham Press, 2014) s.v. "seeking."

CHAPTER 8: YOU STOP WORKING AND YOU START WATCHING

1. Damon, "25 Ancient Greek Inventions We Still Use," History Things, April 26, 2020, https://historythings.com/25-ancient-greek-inventions-still-used-today/.

2. Mary Bellis, "The History of Concrete and Cement," ThoughtCo., March 6, 2019, https://www.thoughtco.com/history-of-concrete-and-cement-1991653.

3. "History of the Greek Cement Industry," Hellenic Cement Industry Association, http://www.hcia.gr/en/compay/greek-cement/.

4. Muzore, Urban Dictionary, s.v. "Greek broom," October 5, 2017, https://www.urbandictionary.com/define.php?term=Greek%20broom.

5. Daveyyyy10, Urban Dictionary, s.v. "Mediterranean Broom," December 6, 2011, https://www.urbandictionary.com/define.php ?term=Mediterranean%20Broom.

6. Stephen Mattson, "Jesus Was a Protester," *Sojourners*, March 16, 2016, https://sojo.net/articles/jesus-was-protester.

7. Caine, 20/20: Seen. Chosen. Sent. (Nashville: Lifeway, 2019), 171.

8. Caine, 175.

9. Caine, 60.

CHAPTER 9: YOU STOP PRESSING AND YOU START COASTING

1. "The Legend of Cliff Young: The 61 Year Old Farmer Who Won the World's Toughest Race," Elite Feet, https://elitefeet.com/the-legend -of-cliff-young/; Daven Hiskey, "A 61 Year Old Potato Farmer Once Won One of the World's Most Grueling Athletic Competitions," Today I Found Out, October 27, 2011, https://www.todayifoundout .com/index.php/2011/10/a-61-year-old-potato-farmer-once-won -one-of-the-worlds-most-grueling-athletic-competitions/.

2. W. E. Vine, Vine's Expository Dictionary of Old and New Testament Words (Grand Rapids: Revell, 1981), s.v. "dioko."

3. *Merriam-Webster*, s.v. "coast (v.)," https://www.merriam-webster .com/dictionary/coast.

4. Kenton and Jane, "Greek Olive Oil: An Overview of the Olive Oils from Greece," *Lemon & Olives* (blog), https://www.lemonandolives .com/greek-olive-oil-an-overview-of-the-olive-oils-from-greece/.

5. *Merriam-Webster*, s.v. "endurance," https://www.merriam-webster .com/dictionary/endurance.

6. *Vine's Expository Dictionary*, s.v. "hupomone."

CONCLUSION

1. Andrew Knowles, *The Bible Guide* (Minneapolis: Augsburg Fortress, 2002), 394.

2. Rev. Dan McDowell, "The History and Significance of Church Bells," *Olean Times Herald*, August 1, 2014, https://www.oleantimes herald.com/

search/?l=25&sort=relevance&f=html&t=article%2Cvideo%2
Cyoutube%2Ccollection&app=editorial&nsa=eedition&q=history
+church+bells; Dolores Smyth, "What Is the Origin and Purpose of
Church Bells?," Christianity.com, July 16, 2019, https://www
.christianity.com/wiki/church/what-is-the-origin-and-purpose-of
-church-bells.html.

3. The Brooklyn Paper, "Church Bells Toll in Brooklyn and Queens
Amid Coronavirus Outbreak," QNS, April 3, 2020, https://qns
.com/2020/04/church-bells-toll-in-brooklyn-and-queens-amid
-coronavirus-outbreak/; Jack Wellman, "Why Do Churches Have
Bells?," Patheos, October 28, 2016, https://www.patheos.com
/blogs/christiancrier/2016/10/28/why-do-churches-have-bells/.

4. "Hosemann: Ring Church Bells in Support of Healthcare Workers,"
WJTV, April 3, 2020, https://www.wjtv.com/health/coronavirus
/hosemann-ring-church-bells-in-support-of-healthcare-workers
/; Ellen Ciurczak, "Ring Bells Amid Coronavirus: Mississippi
Churches, Residents Statewide Asked to Join In," Clarion-Ledger,
April 6, 2020, https://www.clarionledger.com/story/news/2020/04
/06/coronavirus-mississippi-churches-residents-ringing-bells-6-p
-m-daily-support-health-care-workers/2954208001/.

5. Jenny Montgomery, "Ringing the Bell Marks a Milestone in
Cancer Treatment," MD Anderson Cancer Center, October 28,
2019, https://www.mdanderson.org/cancerwise/why-do-cancer
-patients-ring-a-bell-after-treatment.h00-159306990.html.

ABOUT THE AUTHOR

Christine Caine is an Australian-born, Greek-blooded lover of Jesus, activist, author, and international speaker. Together with her husband, Nick, she leads the anti–human trafficking organization A21, as well as Propel Women. They and their two daughters make their home in Southern California.